American Heritage Series

Black History Activities

Author:	Schyrlet Cameron
Editor:	Mary Dieterich
Contributor:	Karl Mechem
Proofreaders:	Alexis Fey and Margaret Brown

COPYRIGHT © 2022 Mark Twain Media, Inc.

ISBN 978-1-62223-878-1

Printing No. CD-405077

Mark Twain Media, Inc., Publishers
Distributed by Carson Dellosa Education

Visit us at www.marktwainpublishing.com

Table of Contents

Introduction to the Teacher

Black History Activities is one of several books in Mark Twain Media's American Heritage Series for grades 5 through 8. The content and activities are designed to provide students with opportunities to explore the significant events and people that helped shape our nation.

The study of history is important because if we don't know where we have been, we have no way to understand the present or predict the future. We should not try to hide from the past, even the unpleasant parts, so the bad decisions that were made have been included along with those that brought achievement and growth. Progress for our nation depends on how we as individuals and groups evaluate our decisions and react to the decisions of others. Wise decisions pull us up; foolish decisions push us down. As humans, we are all capable of both.

How the Book is Organized

The book text is presented in an easy-to-read format that does not overwhelm the struggling reader. Vocabulary words are boldfaced. The lessons provide challenging activities that promote reading, critical thinking, and writing skills.

The 28 lessons contained in *Black History Activities* cover five units of study: *Slavery Begins, The War to End Slavery, Reconstruction Brings Change, The Twentieth Century,* and *Achievements.* The units can be used in the order presented or in an order that best fits the classroom or home school curriculum. Teachers can easily differentiate units to address individual learning levels and needs. Each lesson consists of two pages:

- **Reading Selection:** identifies the important events and people in Black history.
- **Activity Page:** checks the reader's reading comprehension.

National and State Standards

Black History Activities promotes current national and state standards. It is written for classroom teachers, parents, and students. It is designed as stand-alone material for classrooms and homeschooling. Also, the book can be used as a supplemental resource to enhance the history curriculum for the classroom, independent study, or home tutorial.

Front Cover Identification:

(Center image) President Barack Obama with 111-year-old Emma Didlake in 2015, believed to be the oldest living U.S. veteran at the time
(Clockwise from top right) Martin Luther King, Jr.,; Rosa Parks; Representative Shirley Chisholm; Louis Armstrong; Jesse Owens; the 369th Infantry Division, New York Army National Guard, known as the Harlem Hellfighters in World War I; Harriet Tubman; depiction of a slave auction

A Historical View of Slavery

Bartolomé de Las Casas was born in about 1484 in Spain.

Slavery, a system where one person is owned as property by another, was practiced throughout much of the world for most of human history. There were several ways a person could become **enslaved**, or made a slave. A person could be captured during a war, convicted of committing a crime, or kidnapped and sold into slavery.

Slavery in Ancient Africa

Slavery played an important role in the history of Africa. The **slave trade**, or the kidnapping, selling, and buying of Africans, became a major part of the economy.

The Arab slave trade began hundreds of years ago. In C.E. 665, Arabs invaded and took over much of northern Africa. Captured Africans were transported across the Sahara and sold at markets along the Mediterranean Sea. These enslaved people were then shipped to the Middle East and Asia and sold.

Europeans arrived in Africa in the 1500s and established their own slave trade. Merchants opened markets along the west coast of Africa. The demand was high, and merchants began to send raiders far inland to capture Africans to be sold at the markets. These enslaved people were then transported to Europe, Central and South America, and the British colonies in North America and sold. Between 1500 and the late 1800s, approximately 12 million Africans were sold in the European markets.

Slavery Comes to the New World

Bartolomé de Las Casas was born in 1484 in Spain. In 1492, **Christopher Columbus** landed on islands in the Caribbean Sea and claimed the region now known as the West Indies for Spain. Bartolomé's father accompanied Columbus on his second voyage to the New World in 1493, and in 1502 Bartolomé and his father settled on the island of Hispaniola. He received an **estate**, or property, on the island. After returning to Spain and studying theology, Las Casas again sailed to the New World in 1512.

Spanish settlers in the West Indies made large profits by exporting tobacco and sugarcane crops to Spain. To raise these crops, the Spanish developed the plantation system. A **plantation** was a large farm. The Spanish forced Native Americans to work their plantations. Casas became appalled by the cruel treatment the native workers suffered. He returned to Spain with a proposal to stop the enslavement and cruelty toward the natives. Looking for an alternative labor source, he suggessted replacing natives with enslaved African workers. King Charles I gave his approval, and in 1518, he issued the first *asiento*, or permit, to import enslaved people from Africa. In later years, Las Casas rejected the enslavement of Africans as well. However, the property owners could not be convinced to give up their enslaved laborers.

South of the Caribbean region lay **Portuguese Brazil**, which brought in Bantus, Sudanese, Kaffirs, Hottentots, and Bushmen as enslaved workers from Africa. Some of the enslaved workers escaped into the interior and formed colonies where they governed themselves. The most famous of these was in northeast Brazil and was called **Palmares**; it was a **sanctuary**, or place of safety, for freedom seekers from 1605 to 1694.

The practice of the Spanish and Portuguese of importing enslaved Africans to work on their farms and estates would be followed by the English settling in North America.

Name: Date:

Activity: Word Meaning

Directions: Use information from the reading selection to complete the page. Write a definition for each word.

1. slavery	**What's the Difference**	enslaved

2. Arab trade of enslaved Africans	**What's the Difference**	European trade of enslaved Africans

3. Christopher Columbus	**What's the Difference**	Bartolomé de Las Casas

4. Portuguese Brazil	**What's the Difference**	Palmares

Jamestown

Enslaved Africans, or those who had been made slaves, were first brought to the British colonies as early as 1619. Eventually, **slavery**, a system where one person is owned as property by another, was practiced in all 13 British colonies. From the sixteenth to nineteenth century, more than 12 million Africans were shipped from West Africa to Europe and the New World and sold into slavery.

A Virginia Tobacco Plantation

Jamestown

Jamestown was the first permanent English settlement in North America. A group of English merchants formed the Virginia Company. The aim was to start trading posts in North America. The company hoped it would make a profit with this new business venture, creating new wealth for the merchants who had **invested** in, or put money in to, the company. In 1606, King James I gave the group permission to establish a colony in the New World.

In 1607, three ships sailed into the Chesapeake Bay. The 104 men and boys on board settled on the shore of a large river and built a fort along with several houses. They named the river James River and the new settlement Jamestown after King James I.

The Jamestown colony began to **prosper**, or do well, when the colonists began to cultivate tobacco. **Tobacco** was a plant native to the Western Hemisphere. Europeans had noticed Native Americans smoking the leaves of the plant, and soon smoking tobacco became all the rage. **John Rolfe** experimented with various types of tobacco, and by 1612, he had developed a type that the English liked. Soon the colony was sending shiploads of tobacco to England. There it became popular and sold for very high prices.

The high price of tobacco created a demand for people to work in the fields. The indentured servant system was used to provide workers for the colony. An **indentured servant** was a person without enough money to pay for the ocean voyage. The person signed a contract for free passage to America. The contract was sold to a farmer or merchant when the person arrived, and in return, the person worked off the cost of the passage. It often took five to seven years of hard work to pay for the trip.

Most indentured servants who first came to work in the tobacco fields were English men and boys. Later both men and women came. For many, it was a way to escape hard times in their country and start over in the New World.

The demand for tobacco eventually became so great the colonists turned to enslaved Africans as a source of labor for their tobacco **plantations**, or large farms. August 20, 1619, a Dutch ship, the **White Lion**, brought 50 enslaved Africans to Jamestown. Twenty were sold as indentured servants. After their time of servitude ended, it is believed that they were freed. This event is considered by many to be the beginning of slavery in the British colonies in North America. Slavery was first recognized by Virginia law in the 1660s.

Name:

Date:

Activity: Cause and Effect

Directions: Use information from the reading selection to complete the graphic organizer.

The Jamestown Settlement

Cause

Effect

1.
In 1606, King James I gives the Virginia Company permission to establish a colony in the New World.

2.
In 1612, John Rolfe experiments with various types of tobacco.

3.
In 1619, a Dutch ship, the *White Lion*, arrives in Jamestown.

The Middle Passage

The Middle Passage

The **Transatlantic slave trade**, sometimes referred to as the triangle trade, was the selling of imprisoned Africans by Europeans in and around the Atlantic Ocean. The trade routes formed a triangle and included three parts in which arms, textiles, and wine were shipped from Europe to Africa, enslaved people from Africa to the Americas, and sugar, coffee, and other raw materials from the Americas to Europe. The **Middle Passage** was the stage of the Atlantic slave trade in which millions of kidnapped Africans were transported to the Americas in ships as part of the triangular slave trade.

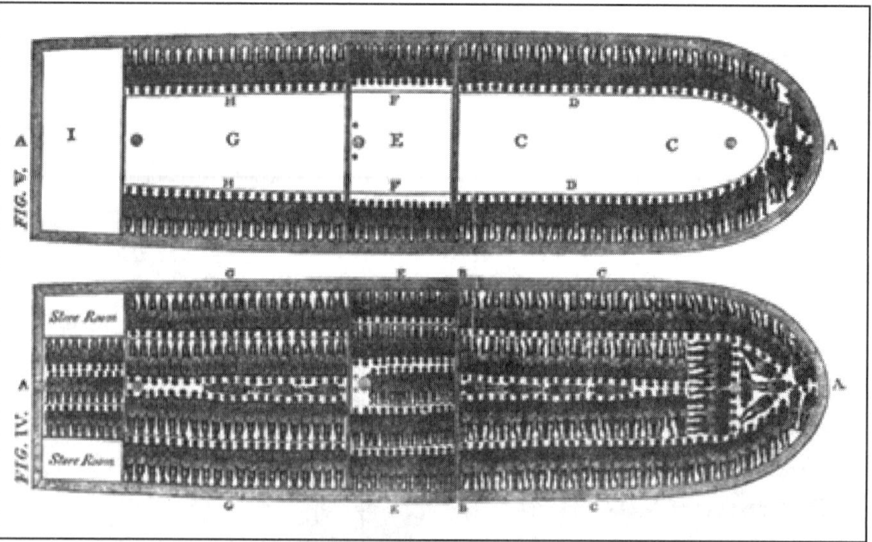

Diagram of a slave ship from the Atlantic slave trade. Enslaved people were packed into the ship as tightly as possible.

The Slave Trade

The African **slave trade**, the capturing, selling, and buying of enslaved persons, began in Africa. Villages were raided in the interior of Africa, where groups of people were captured and forced to march hundreds of miles to the coast. To prevent escape, chains were passed through loops in iron or wooden collars around each captive's neck and through iron cuffs around their wrists and ankles to keep captives chained together. Any person attempting to escape would be severely beaten or killed.

When the captives reached the coast, they were imprisoned until sold. The most desirable Africans were males between the ages of 15 and 25. At Fort Elmina in Ghana, up to a thousand people could be held in stone dungeons. In Angola, captives were penned in open **stockades**, or fenced areas.

After examining the captives and agreeing on a purchase price, **slave traders**, or people who bought and sold enslaved people, usually branded the prisoners with a hot iron to show ownership. The person was then returned to the pens until the trader purchased enough enslaved people to fill their ships.

Ships made large profits by carrying as many people as possible across the Atlantic to sell at auctions in the British colonies. When they were ready to sail, captives were herded onto the ships for the five-week journey across the Atlantic. The prisoners were crowded into small spaces below deck and forced to remain during most of the journey, often chained to each other or to wooden beams.

Water was seldom available for washing. Wooden buckets were used as toilets. It was claimed that the odor of a ship could be smelled five miles away. Because of the crowded conditions, diseases often spread quickly aboard the ships. Historians estimate that in the late 1600s, about one of every four Africans died while crossing the Atlantic Ocean.

Name: _______________________

Date: _______________________

Activity: Central Idea and Key Details

Directions: Use the information from the reading selection to complete the graphic organizer.

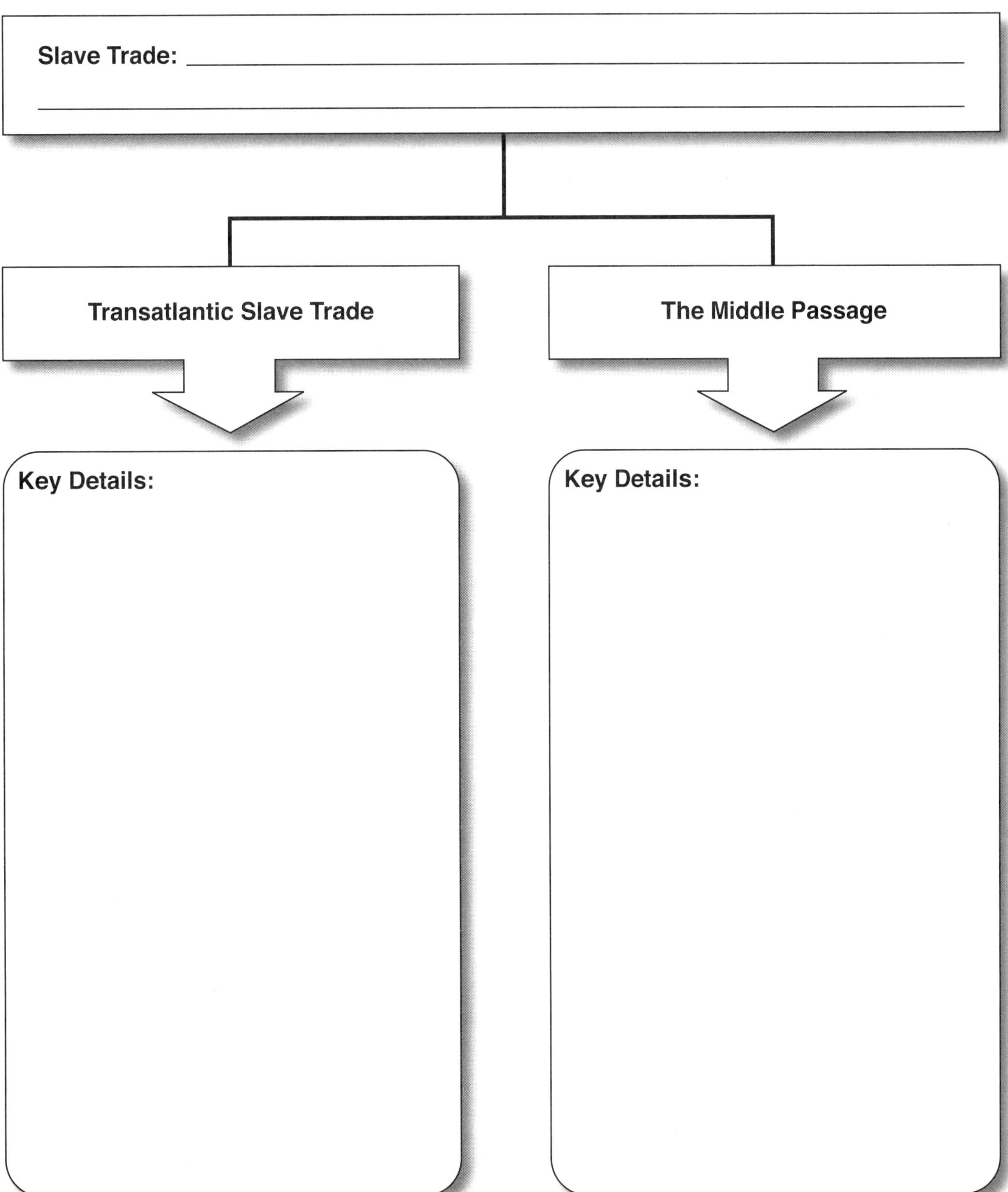

The American Revolution

The American Revolutionary War was fought from 1775 until 1783. It was a time when the British colonists in America rebelled against the rule of Great Britain and King George III. There were many battles fought before the 13 colonies gained their freedom and became the independent country of the United States of America.

George Washington led the Continental Army against the British. About 231,000 men served in the Continental Army. People on the side of the colonists were known as Patriots. It is estimated that between 5,000 and 8,000 free and enslaved Africans participated in the Revolution on the Patriot side.

James Armistead Lafayette was a spy who helped secure American victory during the Revolutionary War.

African Americans in the Revolutionary War

In July 1775, George Washington, a slave owner, took command of the Continental Army. He told recruiters not to enlist Black men, but some were already in the army. In November, Governor Dunmore of Virginia declared that any enslaved person or indentured servant who joined the British Army would be free. Enslaved Africans deserted the plantations and enlisted in the Royal Army. The seriousness of Washington's mistake was made apparent to him when many of the enslaved Africans working on his plantation escaped to join the British Army.

In December 1775, Washington reversed his policy. He ordered that free Blacks could be enlisted in the Continental Army, and most states permitted both enslaved and free Black men to enlist in their militias. Massachusetts and Rhode Island had enough Black volunteers to form separate regiments for them, but in many colonies, Black soldiers served with whites in militia units. New York granted freedom to any enslaved man serving for three years. Two states, Georgia and South Carolina, refused to enlist Black soldiers; even in those states, enslaved men were leaving plantations to serve on one side or the other. Black soldiers participated in every major battle in the war from Breed's Hill to Yorktown.

Two Patriots

In 1767, **William Lee** was purchased by George Washington. Lee served as Washington's personal assistant. He is often shown next to Washington in paintings. When Washington died in 1799, he freed Lee in his will and cited "his faithful services during the Revolutionary War." The will also declared the other 123 individuals owned by George Washington were to be freed upon his wife, Martha Washington's, death. Lee lived at Mount Vernon, George Washington's estate in Virginia, until his death in 1810.

James Armistead Lafayette was an enslaved African American who served as a spy for the Continental Army during the American Revolutionary War under the Marquis de Lafayette. Before the battle of Yorktown, James was able to give Washington and Lafayette information on the location of the British Army's reinforcements. In 1787, with the help of Lafayette, James was granted his freedom for service during the Revolution. He then took the last name Lafayette in honor of the Marquis. After the war, James lived as a farmer near Richmond, Virginia. He married and had several children. At one time, James Armistead Lafayette owned several slaves. Many of these may have been family members he hoped to protect and eventually free.

Name: Date:

Activity: Locating Information

Direction: Use information from the reading selection to complete the page.

Activity 1

What event caused George Washington to change his mind about recruiting Black men for the Continental Army? Use details and examples to support your answer.

Activity 2

How were the Patriots alike? How were they different?

William Lee and James Armistead Lafayette

Alike   Different

The Founding Documents

The Declaration of Independence, the Articles of Confederation, and the Constitution are the **founding documents** of the United States of America. These documents define the framework and powers of the federal government.

The Declaration of Independence

The **Declaration of Independence** is a document approved by the **Continental Congress**, or representatives of the 13 colonies, on July 4, 1776. It officially declared the separation of the colonies from Great Britain. Of the 56 signers of the document, the majority owned slaves.

The members of Congress appointed Thomas Jefferson, a lifelong slave owner, to write the Declaration of Independence. Jefferson listed complaints against King George III, including his belief that the king made slavery possible. The copy submitted to Congress called slavery an "abominable crime." Fearful of dividing the fragile new nation over the issue of slavery, the statement was removed.

The final draft of the Declaration of Independence sent to King George III included these words: "*...all men are created equal...*" The phrase "all men" did not include enslaved or free African American men, Native American men, or women of any race and nationality.

The Articles of Confederation

The **Articles of Confederation** served as the nation's first **constitution**, a framework for a national government, from 1781 to 1789. It was an agreement among the 13 original states of the United States of America. The new nation faced many troubling issues, including the expansion of slavery. To get the Articles of Confederation passed, members of the Confederation Congress made **compromises**, or agreements to give in on certain items by both sides. The members agreed to leave the power to regulate slavery to the individual states. The **Northwest Ordinance** was passed in 1787 by the new government. It declared slavery should not exist in territories north of the Ohio River. However, any enslaved person escaping to the region could be reclaimed by the owners.

The United States Constitution

In 1787, 55 delegates met in Philadelphia to write a new constitution. Seventeen were lifelong slave owners. Many compromises were made before the **Constitution of the United States** was **ratified**, or approved, in 1788.

The South feared enslaved Africans would be counted as persons for taxation purposes. The number of representatives in Congress each state was allowed was based on the number of people living in the state. The North opposed counting enslaved people. The **Three-Fifths Compromise** was reached for both taxation and representation. It declared "all other persons" (enslaved persons) would count as three-fifths of a person.

The North wanted to end the importation of enslaved Africans. South Carolina and Georgia did not want to end the practice. A compromise was reached, allowing the trade of enslaved Africans to continue another 20 years.

Many Northern states had abolished slavery. Southern States feared the North would become a safe haven for freedom seekers who wanted to escape slavery. Article IV, Section 2 of the Constitution known as the "**Fugitive Slave Clause**," declared states were to return "fugitives" to the state from which they fled.

Name: _______________ Date: _______________

Activity: Textual Evidence

Directions: Use the information from the reading selection to answer the questions. Support your answers with specific details and examples.

1. What are founding documents?

2. What are the three founding documents of the United States?

3. Why wasn't slavery addressed in the final draft of the Declaration of Independence?

4. What compromise was made to get the Articles of Confederation passed by members of the Confederation Congress?

5. What compromises were made to get the Constitution of the United States ratified?

Two Remarkable African Americans

Many African Americans sought to improve their lives, whether enslaved or born free in the colonies. Phillis Wheatley and Benjamin Banneker are two people whose achievements inspired others.

Phillis Wheatley

Phillis Wheatley was the first Black woman in America to have her work published. She is remembered as "the mother of Black literature in America." Wheatley was born in West Africa in 1753. In 1761, she was sold to a trader by a tribal chief. Phillis was taken to the British Colony of Massachusetts on a slave ship called *The Phillis*. After arriving in Boston, she was sold to John Wheatley as a servant for his wife. The Wheatleys named Phillis after the ship that had transported her to America. She was given their last name Wheatley, a common custom for naming enslaved people.

Phillis was taught to read and write. By the age of 12, she was reading Greek and Latin classics. It was in poetry that she excelled. At the age of 14, she wrote her first poem, "To the University of Cambridge, in New England." When Phillis was about 17, Mrs. Wheatley gathered some of her poetry for a book, which was published in England in 1773. The book was very popular, and Phillis was invited to England. In England, she was a popular guest in literary circles. After she returned from England, the Wheatleys **emancipated**, or freed, Phillis.

During the Revolutionary War, Wheatley wrote the poem "His Excellency General Washington." She sent the poem to George Washington in a letter. Although busy with the war, Washington invited her to visit him at his headquarters in Cambridge, Massachusetts.

In 1778, Wheatley married John Peters, a free African American. Phillis died in 1784, at the age of 31.

Benjamin Banneker

Benjamin Banneker was an inventor and writer. He was also one of the first distinguished African American scientists and mathematicians. Banneker was born a freeman in the colony of Maryland in 1731. He grew up on his family's farm. He had little formal education but showed deep interest in both science and mathematics. He often visited a Maryland flour mill owned by George Ellicott. Ellicott lent Benjamin books on science and astronomy. Banneker soon became so knowledgeable he was able to predict a solar eclipse with accuracy. In his early 20s, Banneker designed and built a wooden clock. It was the first clock of its type to be built in the colonies.

In 1789, Banneker began work on an almanac. He sent letters to Thomas Jefferson using his almanac as an example of what an African American could accomplish if given the chance. They corresponded on the subjects of race and slavery. Banneker published his almanac from 1792 to 1797.

The new capital city of the United States was designated as the City of Washington, in the District of Columbia, on July 16, 1790. In 1791, President Washington appointed Pierre L'Enfant to plan the streets for the new city. Benjamin Banneker was one of the people hired to survey the area, often making astronomical calculations to guide the surveyors in setting the boundary stones.

Benjamin Banneker died on October 9, 1806. Although he didn't see an end to slavery in his lifetime, his life and his work was used as an example of what freemen could accomplish.

Name: _________________________________   Date: _______________________

Lewis and Clark Expedition Trivia Quiz

How much do you remember about the Lewis and Clark expedition? Complete the trivia quiz below.

1. Who was Thomas Jefferson's personal secretary in 1801? _______________________

2. From whom did the United States purchase the Louisiana Territory? _______________

3. In what year did the United States purchase the Louisiana Territory? _______________

4. How much did the United States pay for the purchase? _______________________

5. President Jefferson wanted Lewis and Clark to find a _______________ route to the Pacific.

6. The Missouri River joins the _______________________ River at St. Louis, Missouri.

7. In what year did the Lewis and Clark expedition leave St. Louis? _______________

8. What was York's heritage? _______________________________

9. Pierre Cruzatte played the _______________________________.

10. John Shields was a skilled gunsmith and _______________________________.

11. What is the Missouri River's nickname? _______________________

12. Which captain was the better riverboatman? _______________________

13. Which captain was the better naturalist? _______________________

14. In the summer, the Otos and Missouri tribes hunted _______________________.

15. What name did Lewis and Clark give to the place where they had the first council with Native Americans? _______________________

16. Which group of Native Americans tried to control trading between fur traders and the tribes north of them on the Missouri River? _______________________

17. Which tribe let the expedition winter near them in 1804? _______________________

18. Fort Mandan was located near present-day _______________________, North Dakota.

19. What was the name of Sacajawea's son? _______________________

20. The portage around _______________________ took almost a month.

21. The Missouri branched into three rivers at Three Forks. The names of the three rivers were _______________, _______________, and _______________.

22. The expedition needed to obtain _______________ and a guide from the Shoshone.

23. Who was Sacajawea's brother? _______________________

24. The expedition crossed the _______________________ Trail over the Rocky Mountains.

25. The rivers east of the Continental Divide flow to the _______________________ Ocean.

26. The Clearwater River runs into the _______________ River.

27. The Snake River runs into the _______________ River.

28. Give the name of the fort near the mouth of the Columbia River. _______________

29. On the way home, Lewis had a serious clash with the _______________________ tribe.

30. In what year did the expedition arrive back in St. Louis? _______________________

Name: _________________________________ Date: _________________________________

Searching for Lewis and Clark: Word Search Activity

Find and circle these 35 terms in the word search puzzle below. Words are printed forward, backward, horizontally, vertically, and diagonally in the puzzle.

Blackfeet	buffalo	Chinook	Clark	Columbia
Corps	dugout	expedition	Great Falls	grizzly
horses	Jefferson	keelboat	Lewis	Louisiana Purchase
Mandan	Missouri	Native Americans		Nez Percé
Oregon Country		Pacific	pirogue	plains
Pomp	portage	river	Sacajawea	Seaman
Shoshone	Sioux	Snake	trade	Walla Wallas
Yakima	York			

```
A H U X I M O J T D E Y A W B S O N K P S R J
E M E W A S L E E S J B Y A U X E V O N T Q I
A F I N D V A F E M D Z B L O Q N K S D X W N
Y O D K A C F Y F U G F K L E W I S R M T N C
M A P M A Z F O K Z A A T A X J N E H A B G Q
N J M K M Y U R C C V V W W W X J S F K L Q S
S G O S O T B K A T N W P A I B M U L O C C H
I F P P U O A S L M A X O L M J O I E K A N S
O Q I O I S N G B Z M T R L E C R E P Z E N Q
U O G Z E R R I S V A L T A T W Z J V W B O G
X U I S P I O A H O E E A S C R C M N D T W Y
D E R C Z T C G B C S Q G G R E A T F A L L S
J O Q Z O A P L U R T F E L X U D D L Y R Y F
H N L S J R E C P E X P M I S W Z C E V H Q Z
E Y O A S E P L R D N O I T I D E P X E D Y B
J L W S K D A S N A T I V E A M E R I C A N S
N E V Y R I E C E S S R V Y L L V T I F K V B
A A R Z N E I U V O Y X R P N G D W S Y J A A
I T B S Z F F Z T J V K N B A C Z R Z V W W T
J O P P I A Y F S H O S H O N E O B I J J M U
D C S C P U Q D E E Z M I S S O U R I V D T O
W J A Z U G I A L J Y R T N U O C N O G E R O
V P L O U I S I A N A P U R C H A S E Y H R O
```

Name: ___________________   Date: ___________________

Activity: Locating Information

Directions: Use information from the reading selection to complete the graphic organizer.

Phillis Wheatley

Born:

Died:

Accomplishments:

Two African Americans Who Inspired Others

Benjamin Banneker

Born:

Died:

Accomplishments:

Events Leading to War

The two different economic systems used in the North and South caused disagreement over the issue of slavery. The economy of the South was based on agriculture and production of cotton. Large farms called **plantations** used enslaved Africans as the labor force. They were considered property and were forced to work without pay or personal rights. The economy of the North was based on manufacturing and trade. The factories used low-paid immigrants from Europe and Asia. An **immigrant** is a person who moves permanently to another country to find work or for better living conditions.

The cotton gin was a machine that quickly and easily separated cotton fibers from the seeds.

Events Leading Up to War

The demand for cotton by Northern textile mills had an impact on slavery. In 1793, Eli Whitney invented the **cotton gin**, a machine to clean the seeds out of cotton. The invention allowed one person to clean in one day what had taken months to do before. Plantation owners expanded the production of cotton. The increase required more workers.

The **Missouri Compromise** of 1820 was passed in Congress to preserve the balance of power in Congress between slave and free states. A **free state** was a state where slavery was illegal. The Compromise was passed in 1820, admitting Missouri as a slave state and Maine as a free state.

The **Tariff of 1828** was a tax Congress placed on **imported goods**, or goods brought in from other countries. The economy in the Northern states was based on manufacturing. The major goal of the tariff was to protect Northern factories by taxing imports from Europe. The tariff on imports increased the cost of British **textiles**, or cloth. The tariff benefited Northern factories because Americans would now buy cloth produced in the North. The South had an agricultural-based economy. Southerners felt they were harmed directly by having to pay more for imports from Europe.

The issue of slavery became more of a problem at the beginning of the Mexican-American War. In 1846, David Wilmot proposed the **Wilmot Proviso** (plan) to Congress to ban slavery in territory acquired from Mexico. The plan failed after Southerners warned it might lead to **secession**, or states withdrawing from the United States.

The **Compromise of 1850** was a group of laws passed by Congress to resolve disputes over slavery in new territories added to the United States. The compromise admitted California as a free state where slavery was illegal, but the compromise allowed some newly acquired territories to decide on slavery for themselves. Part of the compromise included the **Fugitive Slave Act**, which required enslaved people who had escaped (fugitives) to be returned to the slave owners, even if they were in a free state.

In 1854, Senator Stephen Douglas proposed the **Kansas-Nebraska Act** to Congress. The law created two new territories: Kansas and Nebraska. Each had the option to allow slavery if the settlers of the new territories chose to make it legal. Many Northerners protested that this violated the Missouri Compromise, which barred slavery from that region.

Name: Date:

Activity: Event and Effect

Directions: Use information from the reading selection to complete the graphic organizer.

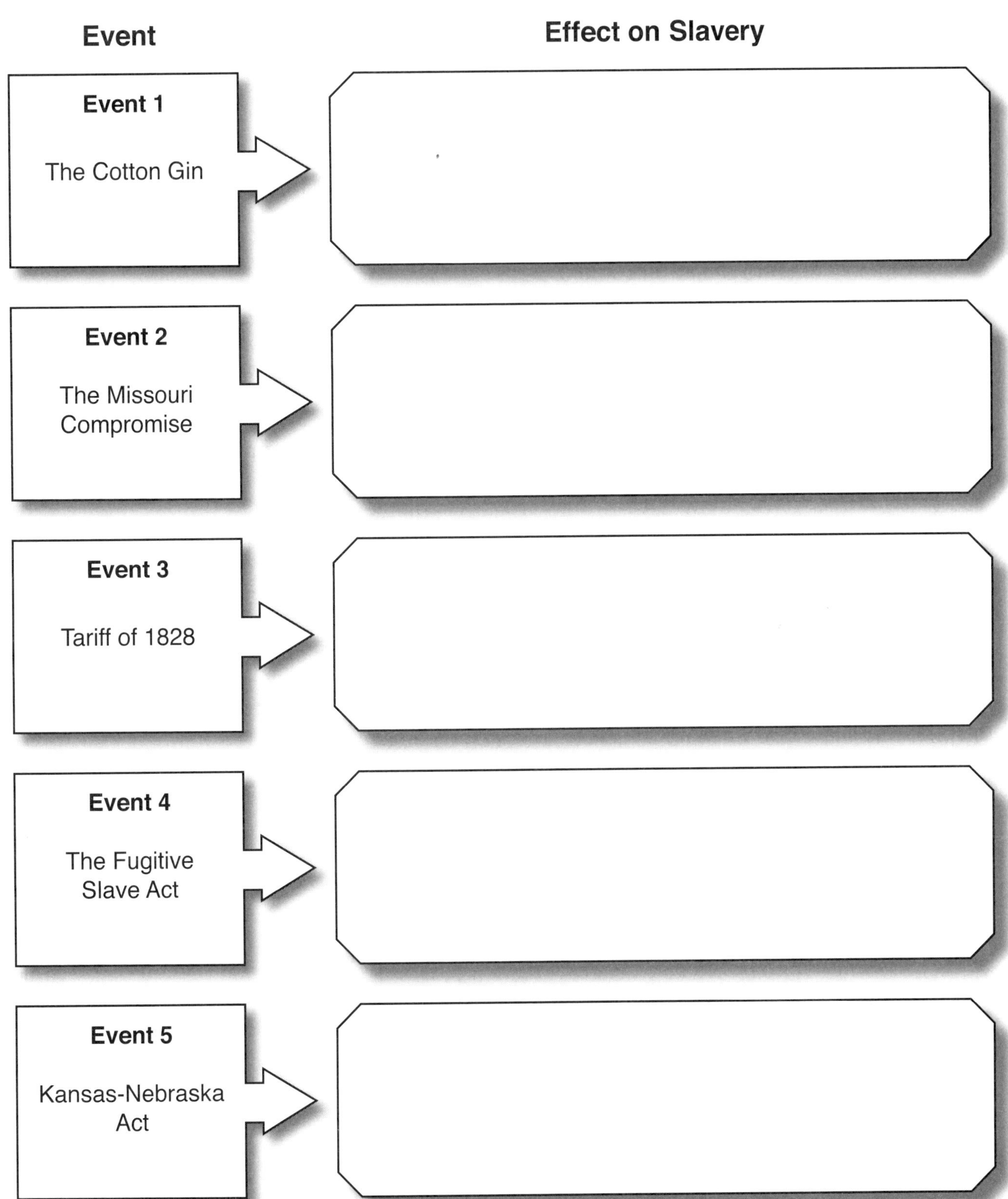

The Abolitionist Movement

The **abolitionist movement** was an organized effort to end the practice of slavery in the United States. An important event in the beginning of the movement was the publication in 1827 of the "Appeal to the Colored Citizens of the World," attacking the plan to settle free Black Americans in Africa as an alternative to **emancipation**, or freedom, in the United States. This text was written by David Walker, the son of an enslaved man and a free Black woman.

Sojourner Truth was a formerly enslaved woman who became an American abolitionist.

Abolitionists

Abolitionists were people who wanted to end slavery. Most early abolitionists were white, religious Americans, but some of the most prominent leaders of the movement were also Black men and women who had escaped from slavery.

The Society of Friends, or Quakers, of Pennsylvania was the earliest group in America to protest slavery. In 1688, four members of the Society of Friends published the first antislavery resolution in America.

Sojourner Truth was born into slavery around 1797 on a farm in New York. Her birth name was Isabella Baumfree. She later changed her name to Sojourner Truth. Sojourner's life was very hard. She had to work constantly and was sold several times. She ran away and an abolitionist family paid for her freedom in 1827. She became one of the leading abolitionists. She advocated for a Negro State in the west on public lands. Sojourner began to work with abolitionists to bring slavery to an end throughout all of the United States as New York had done in 1828. She also spoke out for women's rights. Sojourner traveled the country telling people what it was like to be enslaved. During the Civil War, she recruited Black soldiers to fight for the Union. She was in the very first group of women inducted into the National Women's Hall of Fame. The Mars rover built by NASA was named *Sojourner* after her. The rover landed on Mars in 1997. It was the first wheeled vehicle to travel on a planet other than Earth.

William Lloyd Garrison was a white Northerner. He became associated with the American Colonization Society, an organization that believed free African Americans should move to a territory on the west coast of Africa. By 1830, Garrison had rejected the colonization idea. He became the co-editor of an antislavery paper started by Benjamin Lundy in Maryland, *The Genius of Universal Emancipation.* On January 1, 1831, Garrison published the first issue of **The Liberator**, his own antislavery newspaper.

Frederick Douglass was born into slavery on a plantation in Maryland. Around the age of 12, he learned to read. Soon he began to teach others how to read. In 1838, he escaped to New York City, then to New Bedford, Massachusetts. He began reading William Lloyd Garrison's *The Liberator.* In 1841, he began to speak to crowds about what it was like to be enslaved. In 1845, Douglas wrote his life story, *Narrative of the Life of Frederick Douglass.* The book became a bestseller. In 1847, he began publishing an antislavery newspaper known as **The North Star**.

In 1852, **Harriet Beecher Stowe**, a white American author, published the book *Uncle Tom's Cabin* about the difficult lives of enslaved African Americans. Although the book was banned in the South, it sold over 300,000 copies in the first year in the United States. Harriet's book helped readers see slavery as an unjust and cruel practice.

Activity: Compare and Contrast

Directions: Use the information from the reading selection to complete the graphic organizer.

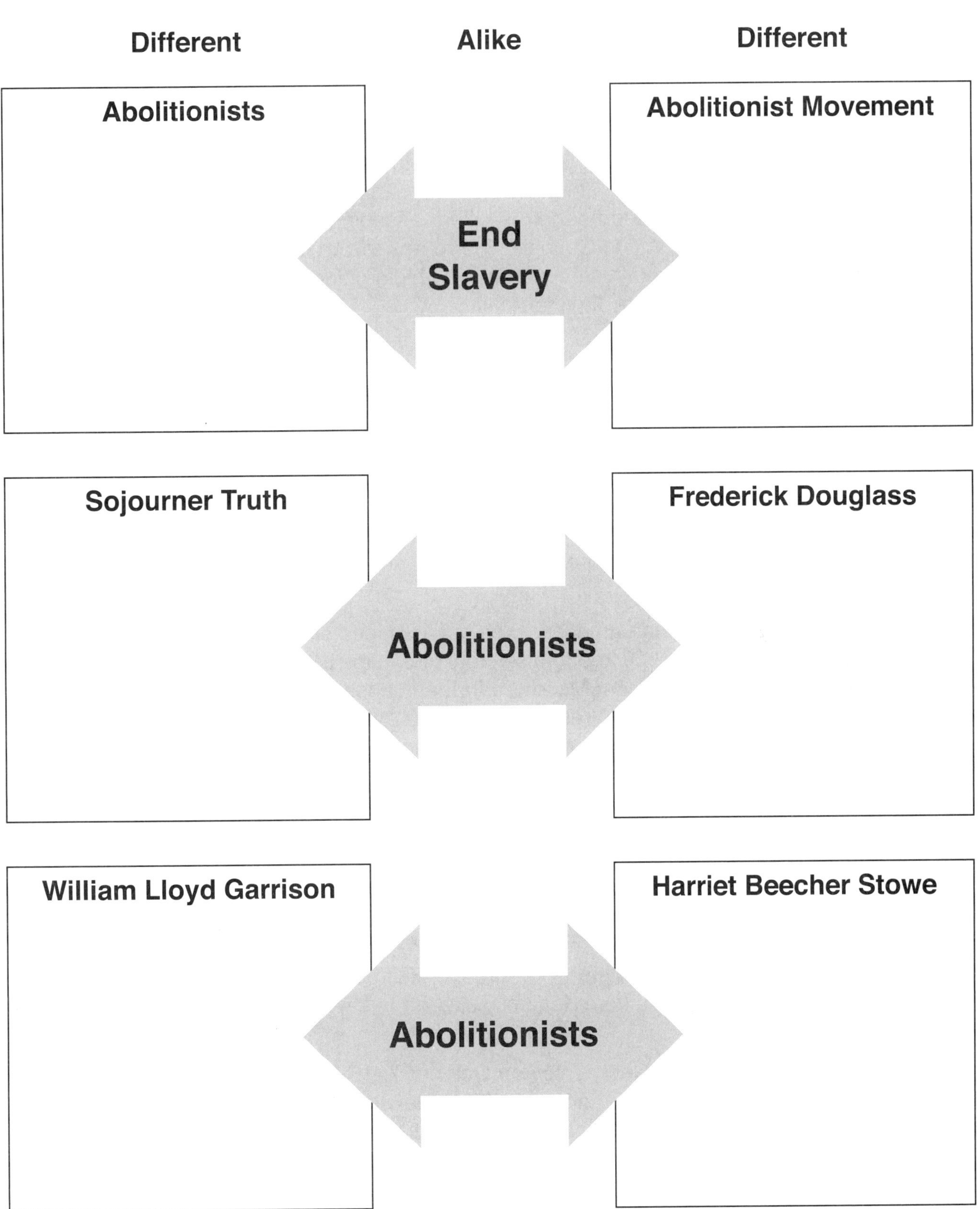

The Underground Railroad

William Still

Some African Americans tried to escape from slavery by running away to the North. The legal term for these freedom seekers was **fugitives**. The **Fugitive Slave Act of 1850** required all citizens to help catch fugitive slaves. Anyone who helped a fugitive could be fined or imprisoned.

Underground Railroad

Despite the Fugitive Slave Law, many enslaved people still tried to escape. A group of people helped them by running the **Underground Railroad**. The railroad was a network of people, African American as well as white, offering shelter and aid to freedom seekers escaping from the South as they tried to get to free states in the North and to Canada. The routes followed were called **freedom trails**. Along the routes, fugitives stayed in safe houses and hiding places called **stations** where they could eat and rest before continuing their journey.

Many of the first whites who became part of the Underground Railroad were **Quakers**, members of a religious group who strongly opposed slavery. Other **abolitionists**, or people who opposed slavery in both the North and South, helped enslaved people escape.

The Underground Railroad was a secret organization. No one knows for sure how many people became part of the organization. Both Black and white men and women became **conductors**, guiding freedom seekers along the freedom trails. Others were **station masters**, hiding fugitives and arranging safe passage to freedom. Escaping enslaved people were often referred to as **passengers**. About 75,000 people escaped slavery with the help of conductors and station masters on the Underground Railroad.

Conductors

Josiah Henson, an African American who had escaped slavery, was a conductor on the Underground Railroad, helping 118 freedom seekers to escape to freedom in Canada, where he established his own settlement. **John Mason**, a formerly enslaved man who had escaped from Kentucky, left the safety of Canada to rescue over 1,300 enslaved people.

Harriet Tubman was born into slavery on a Maryland plantation around 1820. When Harriet learned that her owner planned to sell her, she escaped and headed north. She worked her way along the Underground Railroad to Pennsylvania, where slavery was illegal. After she was free, Harriet made at least 13 trips into slave-holding states and led at least 70 freedom seekers to freedom.

John Parker was born into slavery in Virginia. At the age of eight, he was sold to a doctor in Alabama. He learned to read, and after many years, he was able to buy his freedom with the money he earned doing extra work in an iron foundry. He moved and bought a house along the Ohio River. John became active in the Underground Railroad. He routinely rowed across the river and helped freedom seekers from Kentucky escape to the North.

Station Master

William Still was born in New Jersey on October 7, 1821, to formerly enslaved parents. Between 1844 and 1865, Still helped at least 800 enslaved people pass through Philadelphia to escape to freedom. He interviewed each person and kept thorough and detailed records. In 1872, he shared the information in his book *The Underground Railroad.* After publishing the book, William Still became known as the "Father" of the Underground Railroad. Today, his book is considered an important primary source of African American history.

Name: Date:

Activity: Textual Evidence

Directions: Use information from the reading selection to complete the graphic organizer. Support your answers with specific details and examples.

1. What did the Fugitive Slave Act of 1850 require all citizens to do?

2. What was the Underground Railroad and how did it work?

The Underground Railroad

3. What was the difference between an Underground Railroad conductor and a station master?

4. Why is William Still considered the "Father" of the Underground Railroad?

Dred Scott to John Brown

Dred Scott was an enslaved African American seeking freedom.

Between 1857 and 1859, several events deepened the divide between the North and the South. Each event propelled the nation closer to war.

Dred Scott v. Sandford Supreme Court Case

In 1857, the United States Supreme Court handed down one of its most controversial decisions: **Dred Scott v. Sandford**. The *Dred Scott* case concerned an enslaved African American. He was bought in Missouri, a slave state, and taken into territory declared free by the Missouri Compromise. Scott and his supporters felt this made him a free man, but the Missouri Supreme Court said it did not, and the case was appealed to the U.S. Supreme Court. Chief Justice Roger Taney handed down the majority decision. He said that Scott was not a citizen of Missouri or the United States. The Court also ruled that Congress lacked the power to ban slavery in the United States. The ruling angered many Northerners, increasing tensions and pushing the country closer toward the outbreak of war.

The Lincoln-Douglas Debates

The Dred Scott issue spilled over into the Illinois election of 1858. Stephen Douglas's term in the Senate was up, and the legislature would vote on whether to keep him or replace him with the Republicans' choice, Abraham Lincoln. One of the biggest differences between Douglas and Lincoln was their views on allowing slavery in the western territories. The two held a series of debates. Douglas argued it was the right of the citizens of a territory to permit or prohibit slavery. Lincoln argued that African Americans were included under the rights given by the Declaration of Independence. He thought that while it was constitutional to allow slavery to spread to the territories, this would lead to slavery being legalized throughout the country. He believed only the federal government had the power to abolish slavery. Douglas won the election. However, the debates drew national attention to slavery and the rights of Black Americans.

John Brown's Raid on Harpers Ferry

John Brown was strongly against slavery. Brown led multiple rebellions and helped countless people escape bondage. He planned to capture the federal **arsenal**, a storage unit for weapons, at **Harpers Ferry**, Virginia. He planned to free the enslaved people in the area and move down the Appalachians, building an army as he went. In 1858, Brown met abolitionist leader and former slave Frederick Douglass to present his plan. Douglass declined to participate in the plan.

Brown attacked Harpers Ferry on October 16, 1859. He captured the town. Brown and his men were surrounded by a force led by Colonel Robert E. Lee. Ten of Brown's men and two of his sons were killed. Brown was captured, convicted of treason, and hanged.

The raid on Harpers Ferry angered the South. Fearful of slave rebellions, the raid convinced Southerners that abolitionists would use any means, including violence, to end slavery.

Name: | Date:

Activity: Summarizing

Directions: Use information from the reading selection to complete the graphic organizer.

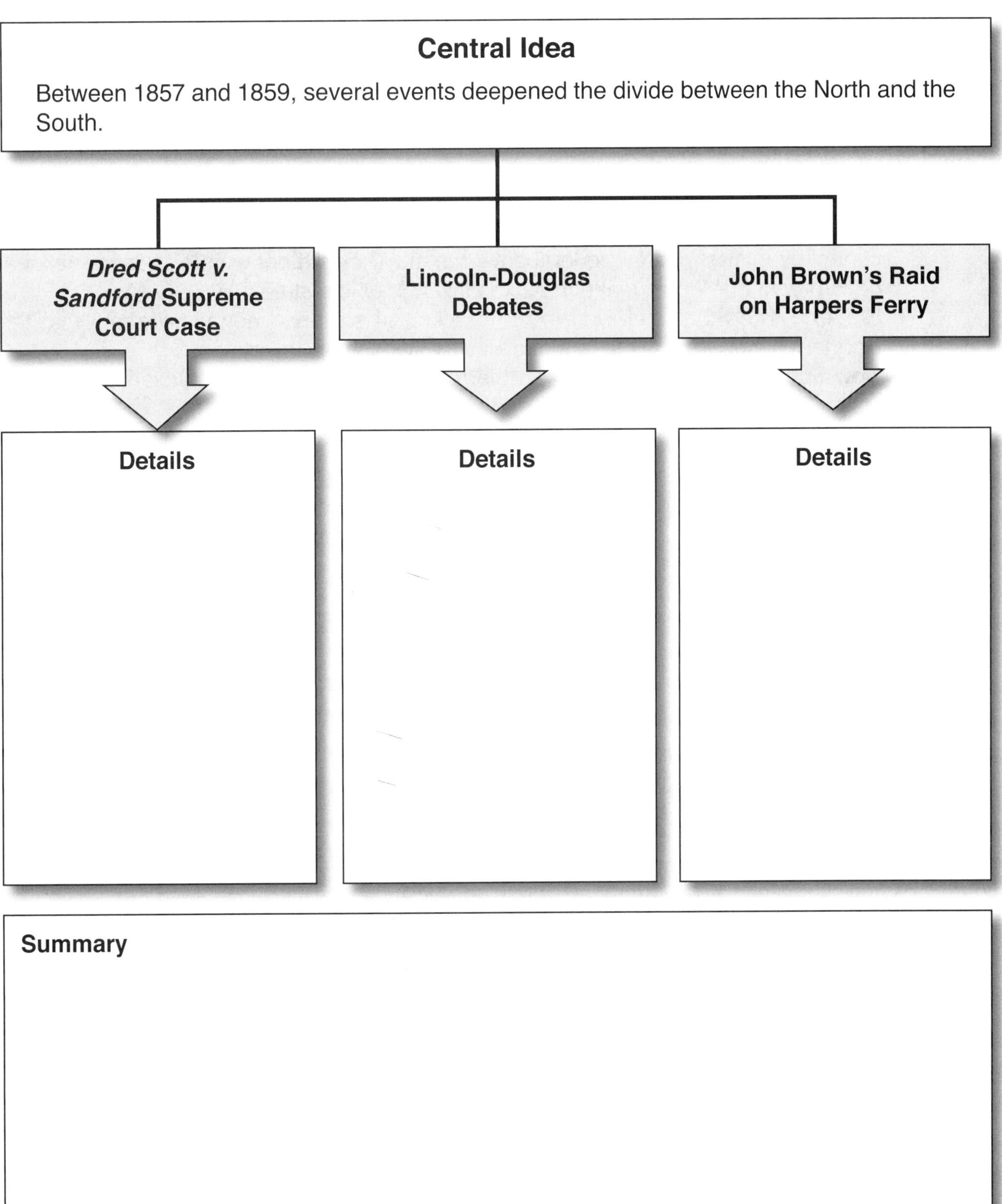

Secession Divides the Nation

Bombardment of Fort Sumter, April 1861

When Abraham Lincoln was elected president in November 1860, there were 33 states in the **Union of the United States of America**. After he took office in 1861, eleven states in the southern part of the country had decided to **secede**, or withdraw, from the Union and form their own country. The new country was named the **Confederate States of America**.

Major Reasons Southern States Seceded

- **States' Rights:** The leaders in the South believed individual states should have more control over laws than the federal government. They did not want a stronger national government that would make the same laws for all the states.
- **Slavery:** The South believed in the practice of slavery. They were afraid that the Northern states would vote to make slavery illegal in all the states.
- **New States:** The leaders of the Southern states wanted to extend slavery into all new states. Northern states wanted to end the expansion of slavery.
- **President Abraham Lincoln:** Lincoln was against the expansion of slavery into new states and wanted a strong federal government, two things the South did not want.

States Secede from the Union

South Carolina seceded from the United States in December 1860. The following year Alabama, Arkansas, Florida, Georgia, Louisiana, Mississippi, North Carolina, Tennessee, Texas, and Virginia joined South Carolina to form the Confederate States of America. They argued the Union was an organization of independent states. Since they chose to join the Union, they could also choose to leave the Union.

Border States

The states between the Northern and Southern States were known as the **Border States**. They included Delaware, Kentucky, Maryland, Missouri, and after 1863, West Virginia. When the Civil War began, slavery was legal in four Border States: Delaware, Maryland, Kentucky, and Missouri, and in the nation's capital, Washington, D.C.

The South expected Kentucky and Missouri to join the Confederacy. In the end, all four states remained with the Union. Kansas joined the Union as a state in January 1861, and part of Virginia separated from the rest of the state to become West Virginia, a Union state, in 1863.

The War Begins

In 1861, **Jefferson Davis** was elected president of the Confederate States. He immediately ordered all federal troops of the United States to leave all government forts and buildings in Confederate territory. Abraham Lincoln refused to comply with the order and pledged to maintain control of all federal property.

On April 9, 1861, President Davis sent General P.G.T. Beauregard to demand the surrender of **Fort Sumter** in South Carolina, a Confederate state. **Major Robert Anderson** was in command of the Union forces at Fort Sumter when Confederates bombarded the fort on April 12. Anderson surrendered the fort on April 13. The Civil War had begun.

Name: Date:

Activity: Locating Information

Directions: Use information from the reading selection to complete the page.

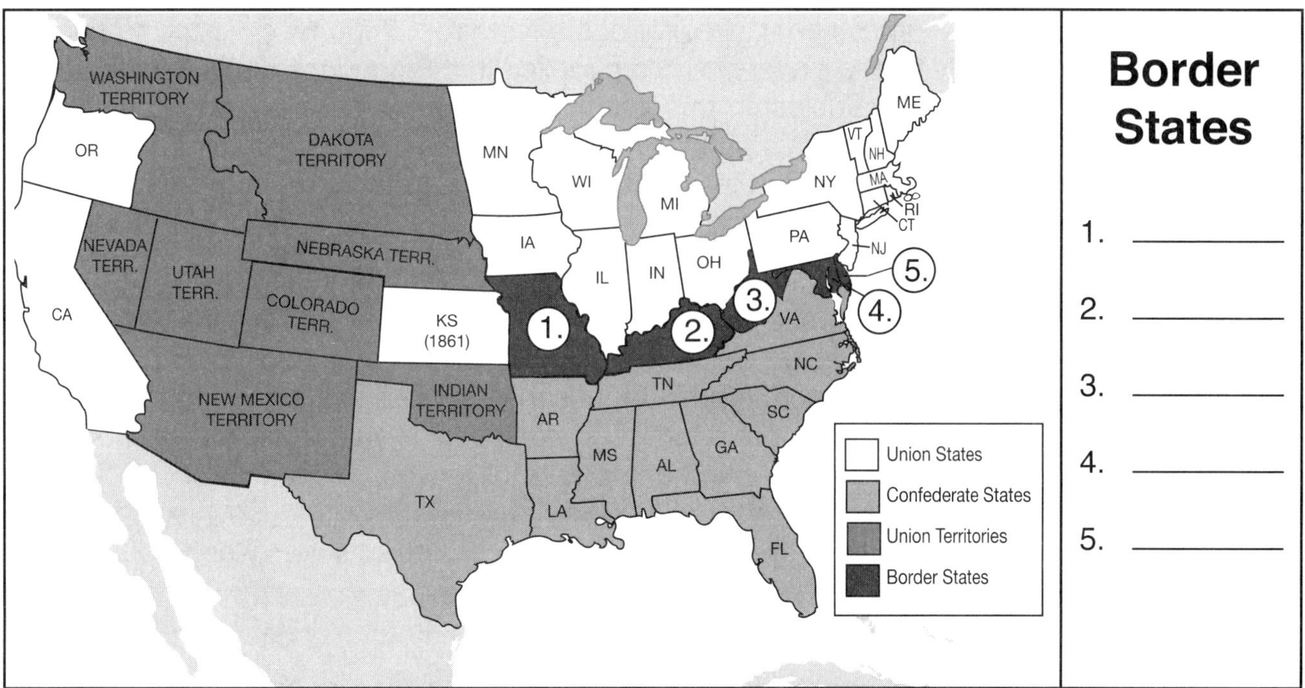

Southern States Secede	
Cause	**Reason**
States' Rights	
Slavery	
New States	
President Abraham Lincoln	

The Emancipation Proclamation

One of the most troubling questions of the Civil War was whether enslaved people should be freed, and when it should be done. In the early stages of the war, Congress said that the purpose of the war was to save the Union, not end slavery. That view was very close to President Lincoln's. In August 1862, Horace Greeley, editor of the New York *Tribune*, criticized Lincoln for his "failure to act effectively to end slavery." Lincoln replied that regardless of his personal wish that slavery end, "My paramount object in this struggle is to save the Union, and is not either to save or to destroy slavery." Lincoln's problem was that in loyal Border States like Missouri, Kentucky, and Maryland slavery was still legal; he could not risk stirring up more opposition in those states.

Colony on the Île à Vache

Northern opinion at the time was as divided as it could possibly be. The old abolitionists were sure that freeing enslaved people was right. Others said to free all enslaved people and send them to Africa or Central America. African Americans opposed this idea, and one, Robert Purvis, bluntly told Lincoln: "Sir, this is our country as much as it is yours, and we will not leave it." Despite protests from free African Americans and abolitionists, President Lincoln tried to establish a colony on an island off the coast of Haiti called the **Île à Vache** (Cow Island). It was a miserable failure, and after many of the "colonists" became ill, the survivors were brought back to the United States.

Amendment V

There were some real legal questions with freeing enslaved people in Union states. **Amendment V** of the Constitution says that private property cannot be taken without just compensation. Enslaved people were considered private property. Lincoln offered a deal to Border State leaders: abolish slavery, and the government will pay $400 for each enslaved person. They turned him down flat. If he could not persuade loyal Border States to abolish slavery, Lincoln decided to justify freeing Confederate slaves as a war measure.

The Emancipation Proclamation

During Lincoln's presidency, he met with many people concerning the issue of slavery. Lincoln and Frederick Douglass, a Black **abolitionist**, or antislavery, leader and formerly enslaved person, met three times. Douglass noted that Lincoln considered him a friend, although at times, Douglass was critical of the president. Douglass argued for complete and immediate emancipation with full civil rights for both men and women. Lincoln did not believe the Constitution gave the federal government the power to abolish slavery, but he did believe it was necessary to free enslaved people in order to save the Union.

On January 1, 1863, President Lincoln issued the **Emancipation Proclamation**, as a war measure that freed enslaved people in all states still at war with the Union. It did not apply to the three million held in slavery in states that had not seceded from the Union. President Lincoln overcame his concerns about the Constitution by justifying the Emancipation Proclamation as a "fit and necessary war measure" to stop the Confederacy's use of enslaved people in the war effort. Lincoln believed using the proclamation as a war measure was the only technically legal way to abolish slavery under the Constitution. The Confederacy ignored the order. African Americans remained enslaved.

Name: Date:

Activity: Opinions

Directions: Use the information from the reading selection to complete the graphic organizer.

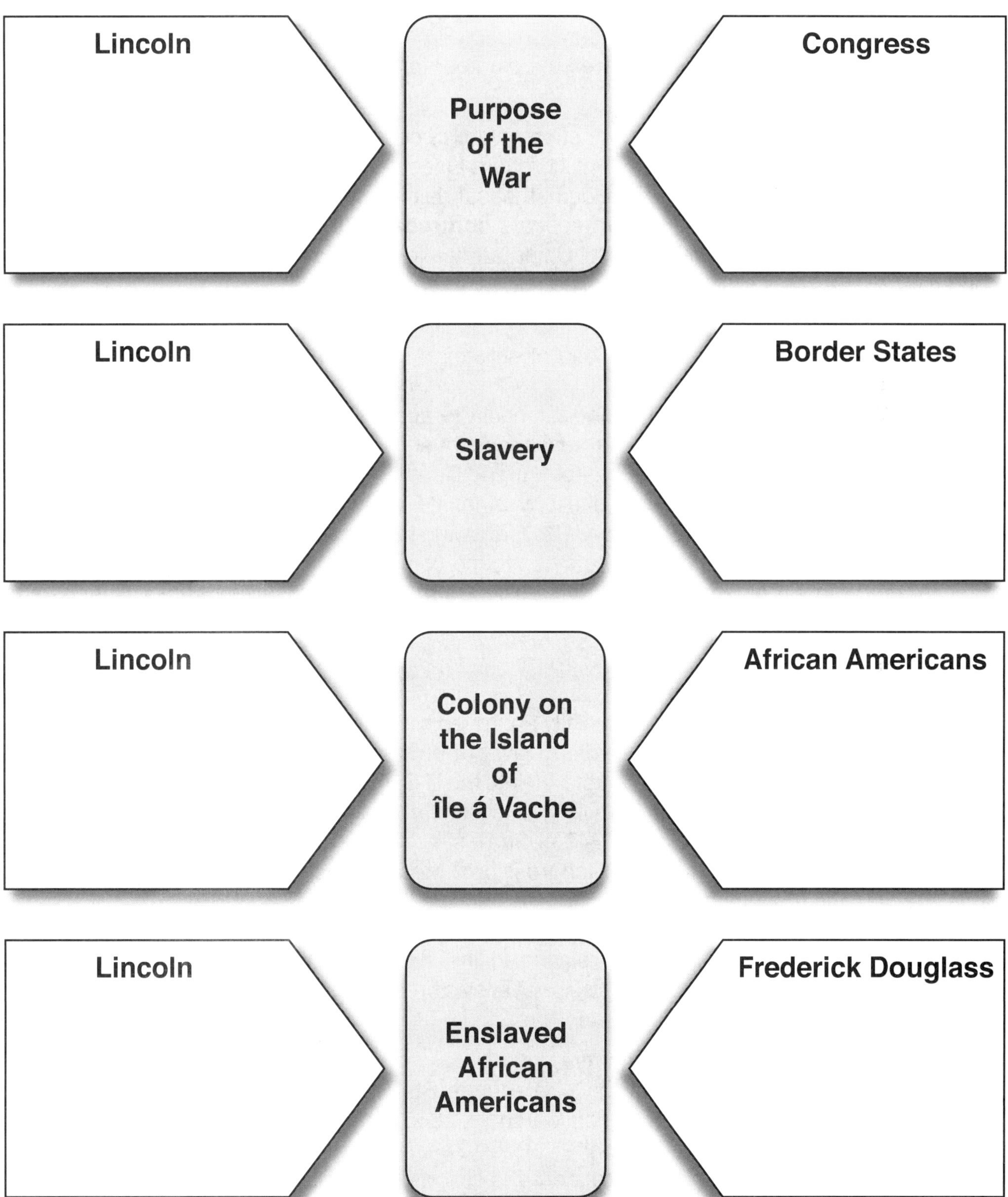

African Americans and the War Effort

In 1861, the free Black population was about 500,000 in the United States; almost half of the population lived in the North. Most of them lived in cities and had developed churches, clubs, and schools. In the South, some free African Americans were prosperous, but most free African Americans in the North and South were poor. From the beginning of the Civil War, African Americans in the North and South offered to volunteer for military service.

Contraband of War

African Americans helped the war effort on both sides. In the North, free Black men wanted to enlist in the army. However, President Abraham Lincoln and many Northerners opposed the idea. As Union armies moved into the South, thousands of enslaved Africans fled to their camps. General Ben Butler called the freedom seekers **contraband of war**, or enemy property. They were often referred to as "contrabands." Union armies in the field began using contrabands as workers.

Militia Act of 1862

President Lincoln opposed the idea of enlisting African Americans to serve in the Union Army. He believed that enlisting Black soldiers would cause the Border States to reject the Union cause. Abolitionists urged President Lincoln to accept Black men as soldiers. Frederick Douglass, an African American who had escaped slavery, questioned this decision. "Why does the government reject the Negro? Is he not a man? Can he not wield a sword, fire a gun, march and countermarch, and obey orders like any other?" Finally, after more than a year of war, Congress passed the **Militia Act of July 1862**, allowing the president to employ Blacks "for any military or naval service for which they may be found competent."

At first, African Americans were only assigned to menial tasks like cleaning latrines and building roads. Before the war ended, more than 186,000 Blacks had fought in the Union Army and participated in over 500 battles.

Black Troops in the Union Army

In January 1863, the first unit officially approved was the **1st South Carolina Volunteers.** It was made up of men who had escaped slavery from the South. The **54th Massachusetts Volunteers Infantry Regiment** was mustered into the U.S. Army on May 13, 1863. The regiment, led by Colonel Robert Shaw, was the first military unit of Black soldiers raised in the North. In 1863 at Fort Wagner, South Carolina, 247 of Shaw's men were killed out of the unit's 600 men. In 1900, William Carney received the Congressional Medal of Honor for his bravery during the battle. He was the first African American to ever receive the honor.

The **Bureau of Colored Troops** was created by the United States War Department on May 22, 1863, to handle "all matters relating to the organization of colored troops." General Lorenzo Thomas was sent to the Mississippi Valley to recruit Black men. He was able to raise 76,000 troops.

Black Troops in the Confederate Army

Jefferson Davis, president of the Confederate States, signed **General Orders, No. 14**, also known as the **Negro Soldier Law**, on March 13, 1865. However, Confederate Black soldiers never fought in the Civil War. On April 9, 1865, General Robert E. Lee, commander of the Confederate Army, and his troops surrendered to Union General Ulysses S. Grant in the village of Appomattox Court House, Virginia, effectively ending the Civil War.

Name: Date:

Activity: Key Details

Directions: Complete the graphic organizer with details from the reading selection.

Key Details

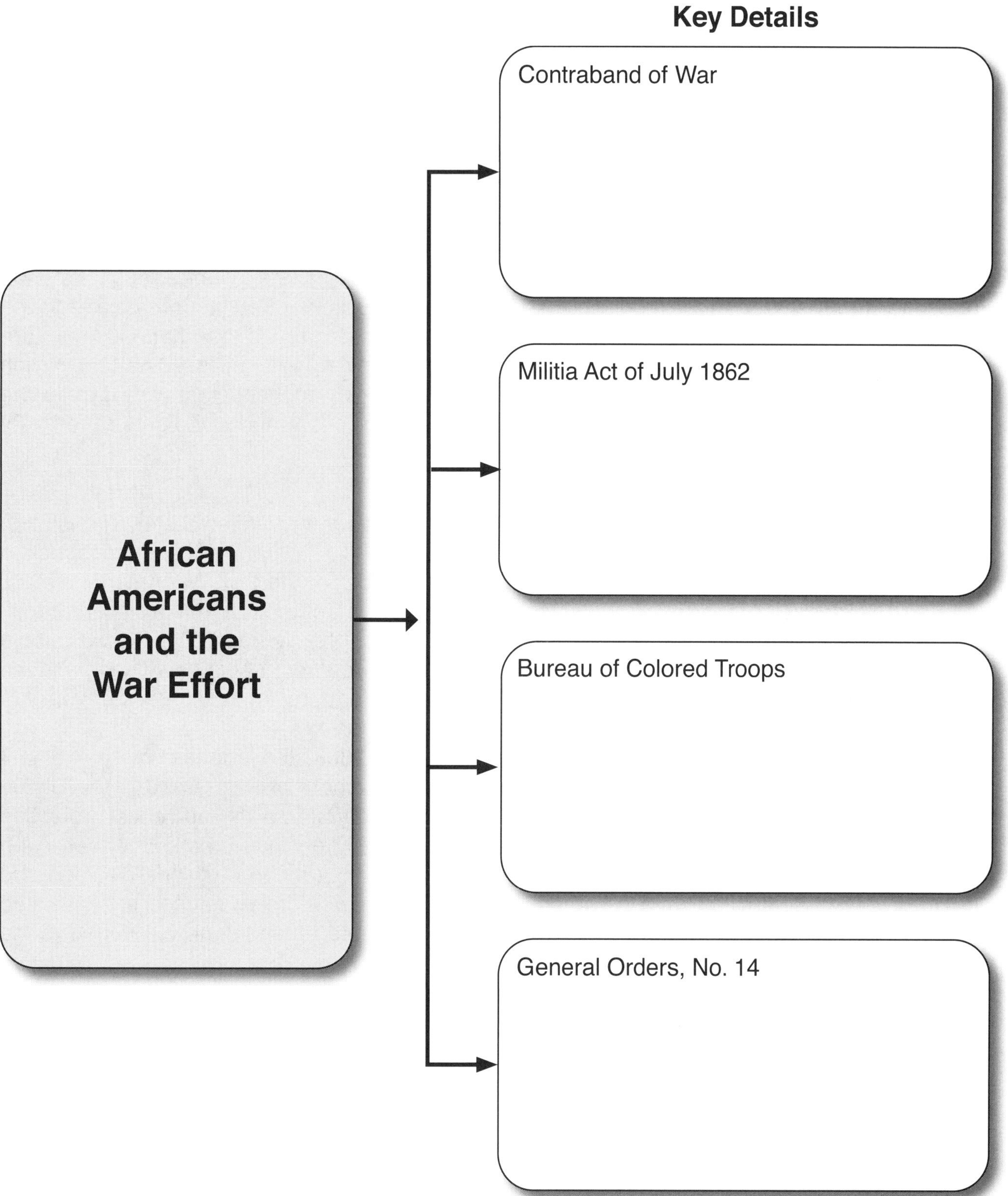

Reconstruction Amendments

When the American Civil War ended in 1865, over 620,000 Americans had died. It is estimated over 360,222 Union soldiers and close to 250,000 Confederate soldiers had been killed. Another 37,000 African Americans died fighting for their freedom.

The Thirteenth, Fourteenth, and Fifteenth Amendments to the United States Constitution were adopted during the Reconstruction Era.

On June 19, 1865, when U.S. General Gordon Granger informed the people of Galveston, Texas, of the Emancipation Proclamation, the celebration that followed came to be known as **Juneteenth**. It is now a federal holiday commemorating the end of slavery and the freedom of the enslaved people.

Reconstruction of the South

After the American Civil War ended in 1865, the United States went through a period known as **Reconstruction**, or rebuilding. The war caused billions of dollars of damage to the South. Cities were in ruins; homes had been burned, crops destroyed, and railroad lines torn up. The Southern economy was ruined. Confederate money was worthless. The four million enslaved African Americans were now free. The purpose of Reconstruction was to help the South become a part of the Union again and ensure the freedom and civil rights of formerly enslaved people.

Reconstruction Amendments

The Thirteenth, Fourteenth, and Fifteenth Amendments to the United States Constitution were adopted between 1865 and 1870. The amendments were a part of the Reconstruction process and are known as the **Reconstruction Amendments**, or the Civil War Amendments.

- **Thirteenth Amendment**: President Lincoln pressed Congress to make slavery illegal. On December 18, 1865, the Thirteenth Amendment finally freed all enslaved people within the United States and made slavery illegal forever. It also gave Congress the power to enforce the amendment. However, the formerly enslaved people were not considered "citizens" and did not have the right to vote.
- **Fourteenth Amendment**: Adopted on July 28, 1868, the Fourteenth Amendment granted citizenship to men over 21 who had been born or naturalized in the United States. It also guaranteed **due process**, or right to a trial by a jury, and equal protection under the law to all citizens. This included formerly enslaved men. However, even though the amendment stated "all persons," it did not mean everyone. Women and Native Americans were excluded. President Andrew Johnson refused to sign it into law. Congress overrode his **veto**, or refusal, and the amendment was added to the Constitution.
- **Fifteenth Amendment**: Although the Fourteenth Amendment gave African American men all rights of citizenship, many were denied those rights, particularly the right to vote. Congress felt it was necessary to add an amendment that specifically stated that all citizens had the right to vote and that no state could deny that right. The Fifteenth Amendment was approved by Congress in the last days of President Johnson's administration. President Grant supported the amendment and worked to get it approved by the states. It was **ratified**, or approved, on February 3, 1870.

Name: ____________________________   Date: ____________________

Activity: Cause and Effect

Directions: Complete the graphic organizer using information from the reading selection.

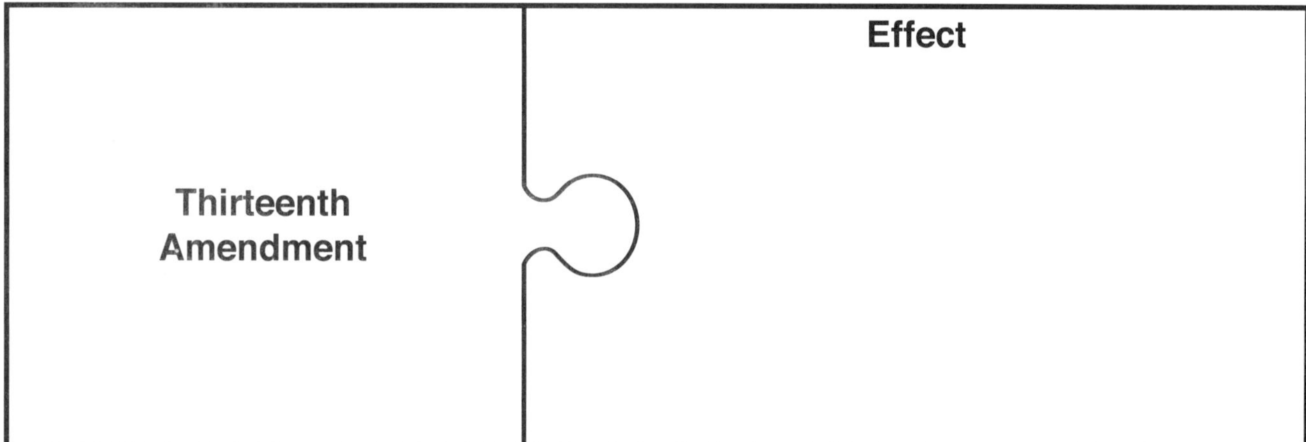

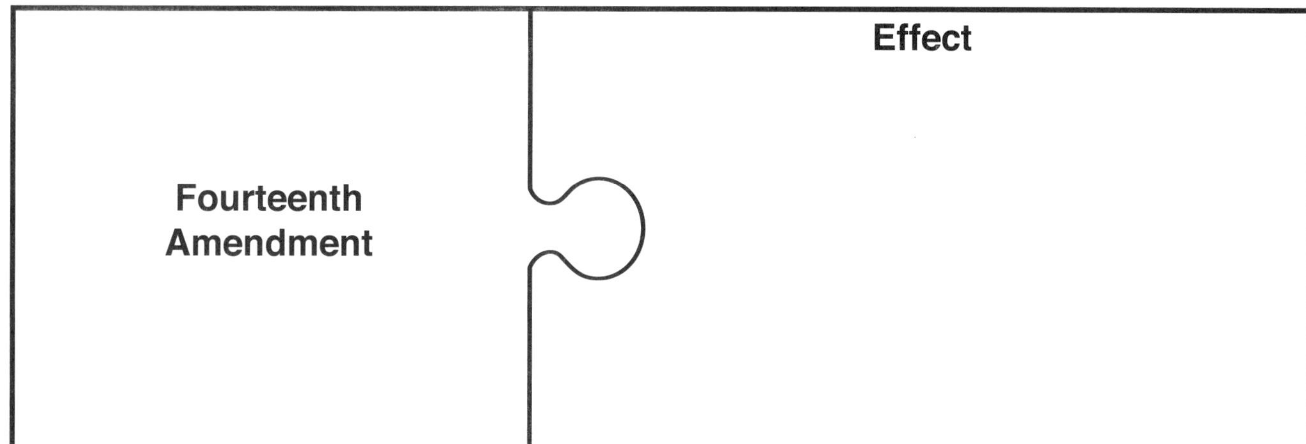

The Freedmen's Bureau

One of the challenges of rebuilding the South after the Civil War was how to help the 4 million **freedmen**, or formerly enslaved people, transition from slavery to freedom. Most had no property, few skills, and nowhere to go. President Abraham Lincoln developed a plan to deal with the problem. He proposed creating a federal agency to assist the newly freed people.

A Freedmen's School in North Carolina in 1866.

Freedmen's Bureau

The **United States Bureau of Refugees, Freedmen, and Abandoned Lands** was established by Congress on March 3, 1865. It was created two months before Robert E. Lee and the Confederate Army surrendered to Ulysses S. Grant at Appomattox Court House in Virginia. The new agency was placed under the authority of the United States War Department. The bureau had the authority to operate for the duration of the war and for one year after. Many of the men who ran the bureau were former Civil War soldiers.

Purpose of the Freedmen's Bureau

By the time the Civil War ended, the **bureau**, or agency, commonly referred to as the **Freedmen's Bureau**, had opened offices throughout the South and had begun providing relief to all Southerners. It provided food, shelter, clothing, and medical services. It opened hospitals and provided medical assistance to millions of people.

The agency had the authority to give land confiscated or abandoned during the war to formerly enslaved people so they could have a home, grow food, and take care of themselves. But President Andrew Johnson, who took over after Lincoln's death, opposed that effort. He gave the abandoned lands to white Southerners pardoned for taking part in the war.

Most Significant Achievement of the Freedmen's Bureau

The most significant achievement of the bureau was the establishment of a public education system in the South for formerly enslaved people. It opened more than 1,000 schools. Students from 5 to 90 years old attended the schools. These schools ran seven days a week, with classes from early morning to late at night. The bureau spent over $400,000 to establish teacher training centers.

Trade schools like Hampton Institute in Virginia opened to prepare freedmen for skilled labor jobs. Colleges were established like Howard University in Washington, D.C., Atlanta University, and Fisk University in Nashville.

Congress Terminates the Freedmen's Bureau

Although it did much to help freedmen of the South, the bureau had inadequate funds and poorly trained personnel. As more and more of the power was drained away from this agency, it eventually did little more than oversee sharecropping arrangements between landowners and freedmen. **Sharecropping** was a system where landowners allowed farmers to rent the land in exchange for a share of the crop. Congress terminated the bureau in July 1872.

Name: Date:

Activity: Key Details

Directions: Complete the graphic organizer using information from the reading selection.

Main Idea

President Abraham Lincoln created a federal agency to assist the 4 million formerly enslaved people transition from slavery to freedom.

**Key Detail 1:
Freedmen's Bureau
Created**

**Key Detail 2:
Purpose of
Freedmen's Bureau**

**Key Detail 3:
Major Achievement
of Freedmen's Bureau**

Black Codes to Civil Rights Acts

The Reconstruction Era lasted from 1865 to 1877. It marked a significant chapter in the history of civil rights in the United States. **Civil rights** are opportunities, treatment, and protection for every citizen as guaranteed in the Constitution.

"White" and "Jim Crow" railcars; racial segregation in the United States as depicted in a cartoon by John McCutcheon, 1904.

Civil Rights Bill of 1866

The **Civil Rights Bill of 1866** was written by United States Senator Lyman Trumbull for the purpose of giving **freedmen**, or formerly enslaved people, certain basic **rights**, or freedoms, and to guarantee protection for those rights. Many members of Congress felt that this was a necessary step after the abolishment of slavery and the end of the Civil War.

Black Codes

Southern states were opposed to the Civil Rights Bill. In 1865 and early 1866, the new Southern state **legislatures**, or lawmaking bodies, passed a series of laws based on the old **slave codes** that had been in effect since early colonial days. The slave codes were laws based on the idea that an enslaved African was property, not a person, and had few or no legal rights. These new laws were called **Black Codes**. The laws were designed to continue providing cheap sources of labor for Southerners and were based on the belief that African Americans were inferior beings. Freedmen were required to sign yearly labor contracts, often with their former owners. Freedmen, unemployed and without a permanent residence, could be declared **vagrants**. Vagrants were arrested and fined. If unable to pay, they were forced to work for white employers to pay off the fine.

Civil Rights Act of 1875

The **Civil Rights Act of 1875** granted equal rights to Blacks in public accommodations. It made discrimination based on color illegal in theaters, hotels, and on railroads and gave Blacks the right to serve on juries. However, that did not stop the South from passing segregation laws known as Jim Crow Laws. **Segregation laws** separate people based on race.

Jim Crow Laws

During the Reconstruction Era, the federal government controlled the southern states. However, after Reconstruction, the state governments regained control. The southern states were opposed to the Civil Rights Acts. In the 1890s, southern state legislatures enacted a new form of Black Codes, called **Jim Crow Laws**. The laws required "separate but equal" status for African Americans. The laws were designed to keep Black and white people apart in public places such as theaters, restaurants, hotels, schools, parks, trains, streetcars, and even restrooms. In reality, rights and public spaces were rarely, if ever, equal for African Americans.

The name "Jim Crow" comes from an African American character in a song from 1832. After the song came out, the term "Jim Crow" was often used as an offensive term to refer to African Americans. Soon, the segregation laws became known as "Jim Crow" laws.

Name:

Date:

Activity: Textual Evidence

Directions: Use information from the reading selection to answer the questions. Support your answers with specific details and examples.

1. What effect did the Civil Rights Act of 1866 have on the South?

2. What effect did the Civil Rights Act of 1875 have on the South?

Sharecropping

Sharecropper in a tobacco field

During the last months of the Civil War, thousands of formerly enslaved people followed General William T. Sherman and Union troops across Georgia and the Carolinas to the Pacific Ocean. In January 1865, in an effort to address the problem of how to care for the refugees, Sherman issued the **Special Field Orders Number 15**. The order was a temporary plan granting each freed family 40 acres of land on the islands and coastal regions of Georgia. The Union Army also donated some of its mules to formerly enslaved people. Word of Sherman's order spread through the South. When the war ended three months later, many **freedmen**, or those who were formerly enslaved, saw the "40 acres and a mule" policy of Sherman as proof that they would be able to own land. The expression "Forty Acres and a Mule" came to symbolize the expectations of those who had been newly freed. They believed the United States Congress would divide up southern plantations and give them to freedmen.

President Andrew Johnson

Andrew Johnson became president in April 1865 following the assassination of Abraham Lincoln. Johnson did not believe that freedmen should get free land. As one of the first acts of his **Restoration** plan in 1865, he ordered all land under federal control be returned to the previous owners. Freedmen and whites living on the land were informed they could sign a labor contract with the previous landowners or be **evicted**, or removed, from the land. These agreements were the beginning of the sharecropping system. Both freedmen and poor white families became sharecroppers. Those who refused were forced off the land by the United States Army.

Sharecroppers

Most of the people who had been enslaved resumed work on plantations owned by whites as sharecroppers. The **sharecroppers** rented 10- to 50-acre plots. In exchange for the use of land, a cabin, supplies, and a mule, sharecroppers agreed to raise a **cash crop** (usually cotton, tobacco, or rice) and give a portion of the crop to their landlord. After the harvest, the landlord paid the sharecropper a share of the profits from the crop, usually one-third to one-half. In this way, the landowners got workers without paying wages, and the sharecroppers got land to work without having to buy it. However, any debts or expenses encountered by the sharecropper had to be taken out of their share of the profits. Most everything from food to shoes came from stores owned by the landlord. A year or two of bad crops could lead to the sharecropper being hopelessly in debt to the landowner.

The Great Migration

In the 1890s and early 1900s, the boll weevil destroyed the cotton crop, causing an economic catastrophe and widespread unemployment in the South. With northern industries needing labor, African Americans moved north in large numbers. By the early 1900s, one-tenth of the African American population had moved to the north in search of better opportunities. The movement has become known as the **Great Migration**. By 1930, over one million African Americans had moved to northern cities such as New York, Philadelphia, Detroit, and Chicago.

Name: ___________________________ Date: ___________________________

Activity: Cause and Effect

Directions: Use information from the reading selection to complete the graphic organizer.

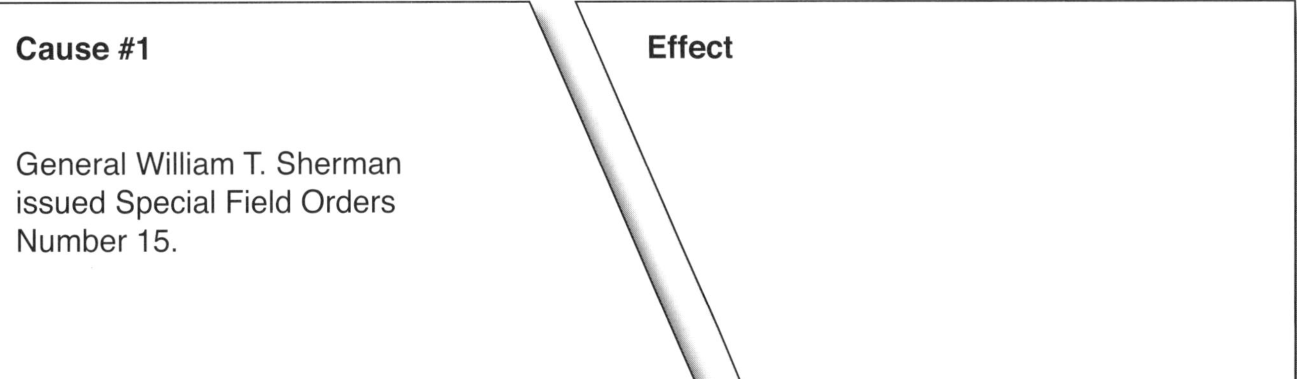

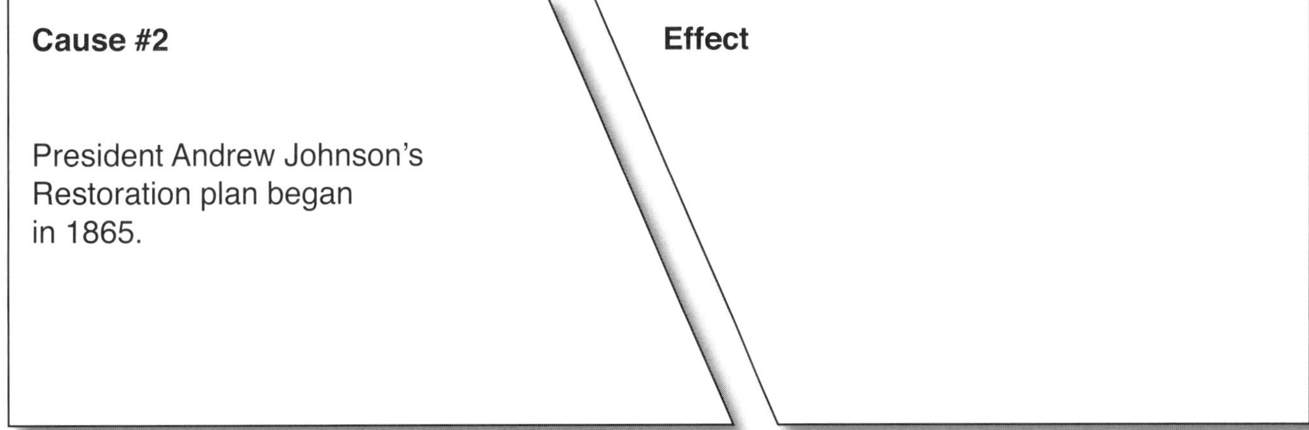

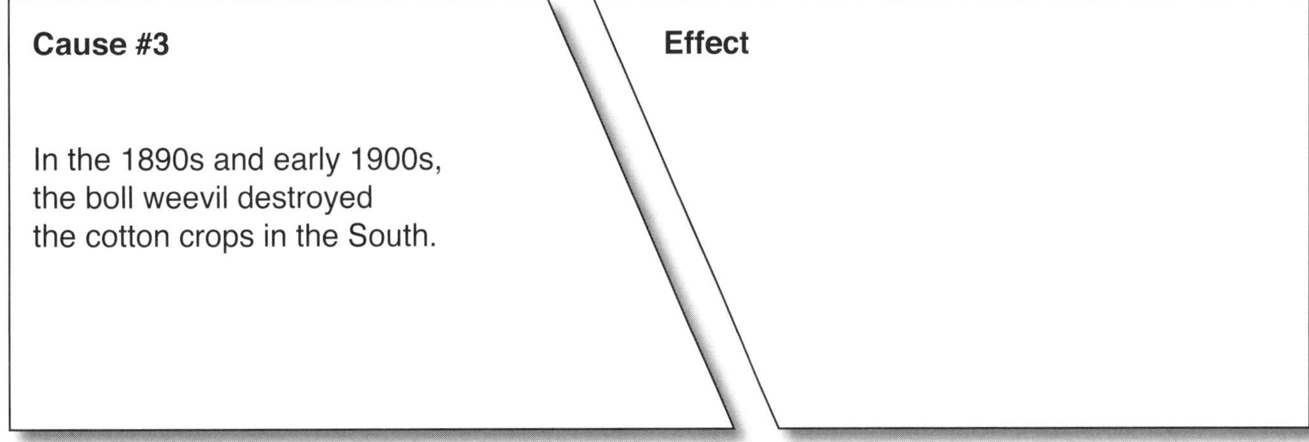

African Americans Move West

In the early days of the American West, the population of African Americans had been low, but that changed over time.

Explorers and Mountain Men

Estevanico was an enslaved African who was the first person born in Africa to arrive in the New World. In 1528, he was part of an expedition to Florida. Eventually he ended up with Cabeza de Vaca on his exploration of the American southwest.

York was an enslaved man owned by explorer William Clark. York accompanied Clark on the Lewis and Clark Expedition of 1804. York was the only African American member of the expedition. He was the first African American to cross the continent and see the Pacific Ocean.

Jim Beckwourth was a fur trapper, explorer, and mountain man. He was born in 1798 in Virginia, the son of an enslaved mother and white father. He was freed by his father in St. Louis in 1824. In 1850, during the California Gold Rush days, he discovered a way through the Sierra Nevada Mountains to California now known as the Beckwourth Pass.

African American Legends of the West

About 5,000 African Americans went west and became cowboys, herding cattle to railway stations in Kansas and Missouri. **Nat Love** was the most famous Black cowboy. He was born into slavery in 1854 in Davidson County, Tennessee. Love's adventures during his cattle driving days became legendary. **Bill Pickett** was another famous African American cowboy. Pickett was born free on December 5, 1870, in Texas. He is credited with inventing the sport of bulldogging.

Mary Fields was born into slavery around 1832. She was freed after the Civil War. In 1895, she became the first African American female star route mail carrier, delivering mail by stagecoach. She earned the nickname "Stagecoach Mary" for her speed of delivery and reliability.

Bass Reeves was a famous Old West lawman. He was born into slavery in 1838 in the Arkansas territory. To obtain his freedom, Reeves escaped to Indian Territory and served with the Union Indian Home Guard Regiments during the Civil War. Reeves became a deputy United States Marshal in 1875 and served for 32 years.

Buffalo Soldiers

In 1866, Congress created the all-African American regiments, the 9th and 10th Cavalries and the 24th and 25th Infantries. The Cheyenne called them "**buffalo soldiers**," because of their curly hair. Among their officers was **Lieutenant Henry Flipper**, who was the first African American to graduate from the United States Military Academy known as West Point.

Exodus of 1879

In 1879, **Benjamin Singleton**, a formerly enslaved man from Tennessee, encouraged people to move to Kansas where officials offered free transportation, land, and supplies for the first year of settlement. Those who moved were called **Exodusters**. Of the Kansas towns built, only Nicodemus remains.

Oklahoma also became a premier haven for African Americans moving westward from 1865 to 1920. By 1890, Oklahoma could claim over 137,000 African American residents living in all-Black towns across Oklahoma. On June 1, 1921, the successful Black neighborhood of Tulsa known as the **Greenwood District** was destroyed when white rioters looted and set fire to the district. As many as 300 African Americans may have been killed, and more than 6,000 were detained for as long as eight days. No one was ever prosecuted for these crimes.

Name: Date:

Activity: Key Details

Directions: Use the information from the reading selection to complete the graphic organizer.

<table>
<tr><td>Estevanico
Key Details:</td><td rowspan="4">African Americans Make a Difference in the West</td><td>York
Key Details:</td></tr>
<tr><td>Jim Beckwourth
Key Details:</td><td>Nat Love
Key Details:</td></tr>
<tr><td>Mary Fields
Key Details:</td><td>Bass Reeves
Key Details:</td></tr>
<tr><td>Lieutenant Henry Flipper
Key Details:</td><td>Benjamin Singleton
Key Details:</td></tr>
</table>

African Americans Who Made a Difference

During the Reconstruction Era, many African Americans worked to improve their lives and the lives of others.

Blanche Kelso Bruce

Blanche Kelso Bruce was born the son of an enslaved mother and white planter father on March 1, 1841, in Virginia. Bruce was well educated as a youth. He escaped to Kansas during the Civil War and became a school teacher. In 1864, he started Missouri's first school for African American children in Hannibal. After the American Civil War, he moved to Mississippi. In 1874, he became the first African American to serve a full term in the U.S. Senate. After his term, Bruce remained in Washington, D.C. He was appointed register of the Treasury and then the recorder of deeds in the District of Columbia. He was also a trustee of Howard University. Bruce died March 17, 1898, in Washington, D.C.

Booker Taliaferro Washington

Booker T. Washington was born into slavery in Franklin County, Virginia, on April 5, 1856. Washington and his mother gained their freedom in 1865, after the end of the American Civil War. They moved to Malden, West Virginia. Washington taught himself the alphabet and studied at a local school. He later attended the Hampton Normal and Agricultural Institute. After graduating in 1875, he became a teacher. In 1881, Washington was selected to head a new school for African Americans in Alabama. The school was called the **Tuskegee Normal and Industrial Institute**. By 1915, Washington had built the institute into a university with about 1,500 students. Many white people admired and honored Washington. He became one of the most powerful African American leaders of his time. In 1901, he became the first African American to publicly dine at the White House after being invited by President Theodore Roosevelt. Washington died in Tuskegee, Alabama, on November 14, 1915.

George Washington Carver

George Washington Carver was born into slavery near Diamond Grove, Missouri, in 1864. He eventually attended Iowa State Agricultural College in Ames, Iowa. He received a bachelor's degree in agriculture in 1894 and a master's degree in 1896. Carver then became head of the agriculture department at the Tuskegee Institute in Alabama. There he stayed for the rest of his career. He gained worldwide respect for his work as a scientist. By developing new ways to process peanuts, soybeans, and sweet potatoes, he helped make them important crops in the southern United States. Carver died in Tuskegee on January 5, 1943. He was buried on the Tuskegee University campus in Tuskegee, Alabama.

Fannie Barrier Williams

Frances "Fannie" Barrier Williams was born free in Brockport, New York, on February 12, 1855. She was the first African American to graduate from the Brockport State Normal School in 1870. In 1893, Fannie helped found the **National League of Colored Women**. Williams worked for the cause of women's suffrage, and in 1907, she was the only African American selected to eulogize Susan B. Anthony at the National American Woman Suffrage Association convention. She spoke and wrote about women's rights and discrimination against African Americans. She helped found the **National Association for the Advancement of Colored People** (NAACP) in 1909. Fannie died in New York on March 4, 1944.

Name: Date:

Activity: Locating Information

Directions: Use information from the reading selection to complete the graphic organizer.

How did each person contribute to improving the lives of African Americans during the Reconstruction Era and beyond?

Blanche Kelso Bruce

Booker T. Washington

George Washington Carver

Fannie Barrier Williams

The Jazz Age

The 1920s is sometimes referred to as the **Age of Jazz**, a time when jazz music became very popular across the United States. People enjoyed listening to it on the radio or going to dance halls and listening to live jazz bands. The music inspired new dances, including the Charleston, the Shimmy, and the Black Bottom.

The Beginning of Jazz

Jazz is a uniquely American style of music that evolved from spirituals, blues, and ragtime.

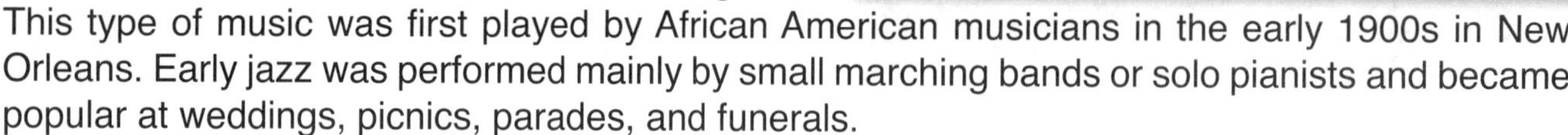

This type of music was first played by African American musicians in the early 1900s in New Orleans. Early jazz was performed mainly by small marching bands or solo pianists and became popular at weddings, picnics, parades, and funerals.

Although jazz developed among African American musicians, no sound recordings remain of the earliest jazz groups. The first jazz recording in 1917 was by an all-white group who called themselves the Original Dixieland Jazz Band. Eventually, New Orleans-style jazz played by white musicians became known as **Dixieland Jazz**.

Jazz in the 1920s involved great experimentation and discovery. Eventually, a Chicago style of jazz evolved, derived from the New Orleans style, but with more emphasis on soloists and often featuring saxophones, pianos, and vocalists. Many New Orleans jazz musicians, including Louis Armstrong, became famous by performing in Chicago nightclubs.

The "blues" was also a style of music developed by African Americans with elements from spirituals, traditional African music, and work songs in a call and response format. **Mamie Smith** had a sudden hit in 1920 with her recording of "Crazy Blues." **Bessie Smith** was the most popular female blues singer during the 1920s. She was known as the "Empress of the Blues."

Louis Armstrong

Louis Armstrong was an African American trumpeter and vocalist. He is considered one of the most influential figures in jazz. Louis Armstrong was born about 1901 in New Orleans. When he was about 13, Louis was sent to the Colored Waif's Home for Boys, where he joined a boys' brass band. With Louis' natural ability for music as a cornet player, he soon became the star of the group. After he left the home, he played in clubs and dance halls in New Orleans.

Louis became friends with **King Oliver**, a famous Black musician. In 1922, Louis joined King Oliver's Creole Jazz Band in Chicago. Two years later, he joined a band in New York where he dazzled both musicians and audiences with his unique loose, springy swing style and his ability to improvise. Previously, most jazz was played by **ensembles**, groups of musicians. Rarely was any one person featured for other than a short solo. Back in Chicago in 1925, Louis led his own band and began making records playing New Orleans-style jazz. The popularity of his short solos soon convinced record companies that he should be featured with other players merely providing backup.

At first, his records featured Louis playing the trumpet. Then he began singing in a rough voice that attracted listeners. His hit songs included "Savoy Blues," "Hotter Than That," "West End Blues," "Blueberry Hill," "Mack the Knife," "Hello, Dolly," and "What a Wonderful World."

Name: Date:

Activity: Key Details

Directions: Use information from the reading selection to complete the graphic organizer.

Age of Jazz

Key Details

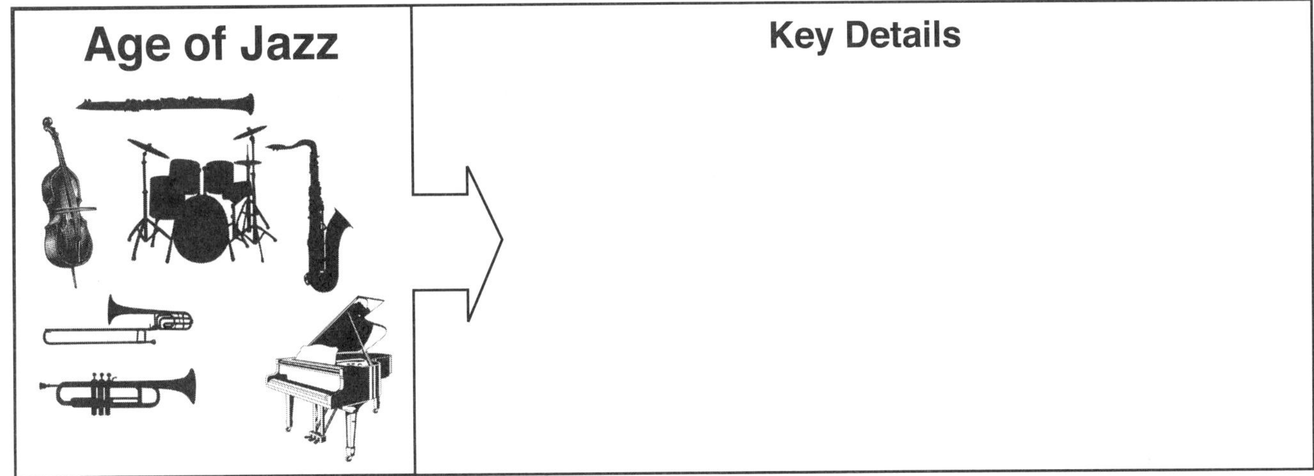

Bessie Smith

Key Details

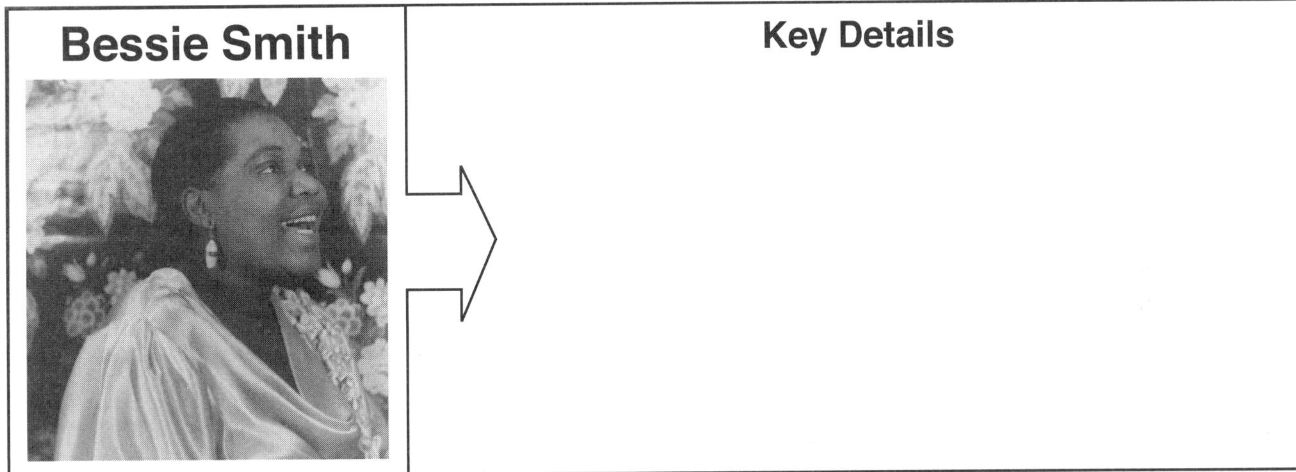

Louis Armstrong

Key Details

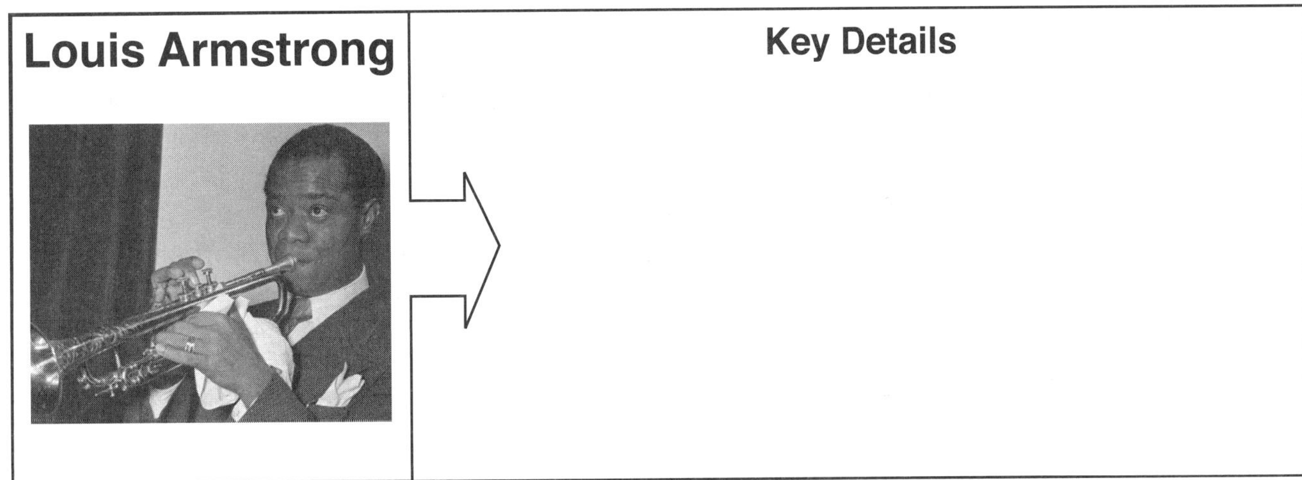

Twentieth Century Wars

The United States was involved in five major wars during the Twentieth Century. African American soldiers fought in each war.

Five Major Wars

World War I began in Europe in 1914. The war pitted the **Central Powers** (Germany, Austria-Hungary, and Turkey) against the **Allied Powers** (France, Great Britain, Russia, Italy, and Japan). The assassination of Austrian Archduke Franz Ferdinand was the main cause of the war. The assassination was traced to a group that wanted to break up the Austro-Hungarian Empire. In 1917, the United States joined the Allied Powers. The war ended in 1918 with the defeat of the Central Powers. The first African American combat troops to see action were the 369th Infantry in France where they were involved in 91 days of combat. The Germans called them **Hell Fighters**, and the French awarded the entire unit the Croix de Guerre (Cross of Honor).

World War II began in 1939 when the **Allied Powers** (Britain, Soviet Union, and France) joined forces against the **Axis Powers** (Germany, Italy, and Japan) who wanted to take over Europe and Asia. In 1941, the United States entered the war on the Allied side after Japanese forces attacked Pearl Harbor, a U.S. naval base in Hawaii. Germany surrendered in May 1945 after Adolf Hitler, dictator of Germany, committed suicide. The war officially ended on September 2, 1945, when Japan formally surrendered following the atomic bombings of Hiroshima and Nagasaki by the United States. About one million African Americans served in the armed forces in World War II. **Benjamin Oliver Davis, Sr.,** was promoted to Brigadier general, the first African American general in American history.

The United States entered the **Korean War** in 1950. The United States and its allies wanted to stop North Korean communists from invading South Korea. The war ended in 1953 in a stalemate. Korea was divided into two countries, North Korea and South Korea. Approximately 600,000 African Americans served in the armed forces. **Charles Rangel** was awarded the Bronze Star for valor and received a Purple Heart. In 1970, he was elected as a Congressman in the United States House of Representatives. In 2007, Rangel became the first African American Chair of the House Ways and Means Committee.

The **Vietnam War** began in 1955 between communist North Vietnam and the government of Southern Vietnam. The United States military entered the war in 1959 to stop the spread of communism in Vietnam. In 1973, President Nixon signed the Paris Peace Accords, ending direct U.S. involvement in the war. The war ended in 1975 when North Vietnam forces seized control of South Vietnam. A total of 300,000 African Americans served in Vietnam. **Private First Class James Anderson, Jr.,** was killed in action on patrol northwest of Quang Tri, saving his comrades from serious injury or death. Anderson received the Medal of Honor for his heroism. Anderson was the first African American Marine ever to receive the award.

The **Persian Gulf War**, also known as Operation Desert Shield/Desert Storm, was fought from 1990 to 1991. The United States led a coalition of 43 nations working together in the Middle East to liberate the country of Kuwait from Iraq. The coalition was victorious in their efforts. About 104,000 African Americans served in the Persian Gulf War. Defense Department statistics show African Americans accounted for nearly 25 percent of the American troops in the Persian Gulf.

Name: Date:

Activity: Locating Information

Directions: Use information from the reading selection to complete the chart.

War	Date	Reason	African American Contribution
World War I	Began: Ended:		
World War II	Began: Ended:		
Korean War	Began: Ended:		
Vietnam War	Began: Ended:		
Persian Gulf War	Began: Ended:		

The Modern Civil Rights Era

Dr. Martin Luther King, Jr.

The modern civil rights movement took place during the 1950s and 1960s. Many African Americans began to challenge Jim Crow Laws. They wanted an end to **segregation**, or the separation of people of different races.

Major Civil Rights Events

On May 17, 1954, the Supreme Court of the United States ruled on the ***Brown v. Board of Education*** case. The court declared segregation in schools was unconstitutional. Many school districts, however, fought the new policy and remained segregated.

On December 1, 1955, **Rosa Parks** was arrested in Montgomery, Alabama, for refusing to give up her seat on a bus to a white passenger. Shortly after, African Americans in Montgomery began to **boycott**, refuse to use, the city's buses.

On September 4, 1957, nine Black students known as the "Little Rock Nine" were blocked from **integrating**, bringing together Blacks and whites, into Little Rock Central High School in Little Rock, Arkansas. President Dwight D. Eisenhower sent U.S. Army soldiers to Little Rock to protect the students.

On February 1, 1960, four African American students refused to leave a Woolworth's lunch counter in Greensboro, North Carolina, that was reserved for white people. This was the beginning of a **"sit-in"** movement throughout the city and in other states protesting businesses that refused service to Blacks.

On April 12, 1963, **Dr. Martin Luther King, Jr.,** led a march in Birmingham, Alabama, to bring national attention to the efforts of local Black leaders to desegregate public facilities in the city. King and large numbers of protestors were jailed. In later protests, the police turned dogs and fire hoses on the demonstrators, including hundreds of schoolchildren.

On August 28, 1963, over 200,000 people participated in the **"March on Washington"** demonstration in Washington, D.C. Dr. Martin Luther King, Jr., gave his "I Have a Dream" speech in front of the Lincoln Memorial.

On July 2, 1964, President Lyndon B. Johnson signed the **Civil Rights Act of 1964**. The law prevented employment discrimination due to race, color, sex, religion, or national origin.

On October 14, 1964, Dr. Martin Luther King, Jr., was awarded the **Nobel Peace Prize** "for his nonviolent struggle for civil rights for the Afro-American population." Although the peaceful protests he led throughout the South were often met with violence, King and his followers continued, and their nonviolent movement gained momentum.

On August 6, 1965, President Johnson signed the **Voting Rights Act of 1965** to prevent the use of discriminatory practices against African Americans at the polls, such as literacy tests as a voting requirement.

On April 4, 1968, Dr. Martin Luther King, Jr., was assassinated on the balcony of his hotel room in Memphis, Tennessee, by James Earl Ray.

On April 11, 1968, President Johnson signed the **Civil Rights Act of 1968**, also known as the **Fair Housing Act**. The new law guaranteed equal housing opportunities regardless of race, religion, or national origin.

Name: Date:

Activity: Chronological Order

Directions: Use the information from the reading selection to create a timeline of the Civil Rights events of the 1900s. Provide an event for each date.

The Civil Rights Era Timeline

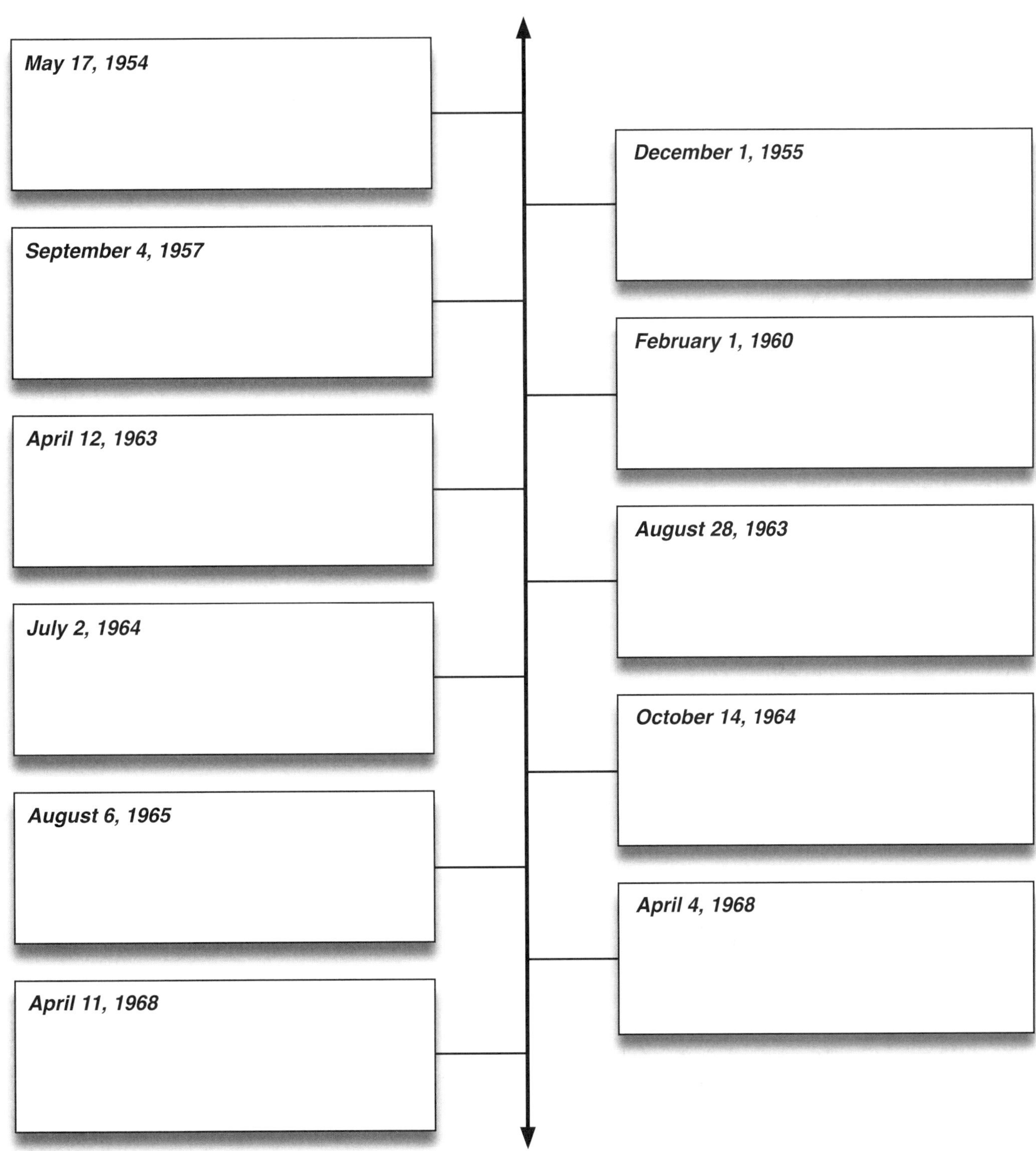

Sports and Entertainment

The role of African Americans in sports and show business plays a major part in American life today.

Firsts in Sports and the Olympics

In 1908, Texan **Jack Johnson** became the first African American world heavyweight boxing champion. He retained the heavyweight title from 1908 to 1915. **Jackie Robinson** became the first African American to play in Major League Baseball (MLB) in 1947. He was selected as the National League MVP in 1949. On July 6, 1957, **Althea Gibson** was the first Black tennis player to win the women's singles tennis title at Wimbledon and became the first African American to win a championship. She was inducted into the International Tennis Hall of Fame in 1971.

African Americans have been exceptional in Olympic competitions. **Jessie Owens** was the son of African American sharecroppers and the grandson of an enslaved person. At the 1936 Olympics in Berlin, Germany, Owens became the first American to win four Olympic gold medals. In the Summer Olympics of 1992, athletes from many nations gathered at Barcelona, Spain, to compete. The U.S. "Dream Team" included many basketball superstars of the NBA: men like **Michael Jordan** and **Magic Johnson**. The "Dream Team" won the gold medal. There were many other stars, including Jackie Joyner-Kersee. **Jackie Joyner-Kersee** is considered one of the greatest track and field athletes in American history. In 1988, she became the first American woman to win an Olympic gold medal in the long jump and in the heptathlon. In 1992, she repeated her gold medal win in the heptathlon.

Entertainment Firsts

In early movies, African American roles were limited yet some performers became well-known. On February 29, 1940, **Hattie McDaniel** won the Academy Award for Best Supporting Actress in *Gone with the Wind*. She was the first African American to win an Oscar.

After World War II, African American actors were featured in major roles in many movies, and stars like **Sidney Poitier** began to make their mark. Movies focusing on African Americans have included such important films as *Raisin in the Sun, The Color Purple,* and *Glory*. In 2002, for the first time, both the Oscars for leading actor and actress went to African American performers: **Denzel Washington** and **Halle Berry**. In 1956, **Nat King Cole** became the first Black star of a national TV show. NBC aired *The Nat King Cole Show* in 1956 and 1957. By the end of the 1980s, many television shows included African Americans in either the leading or important supporting roles.

The African American role in music has become a major part of the entertainment industry. In classical music, for instance, **Marian Anderson** stands out. In 1939, Anderson performed for a crowd of 75,000 at the Lincoln Memorial in Washington, D.C., after being denied the use of Constitution Hall by the Daughters of the American Revolution organization. In 1959, **Ella Fitzgerald** earned two Grammys, making her the first African American woman to win the award. She won Best Individual Jazz Performance and Best Female Vocal Performance. **William James "Count" Basie** became the first African American male to win a Grammy award in 1959. In 1971, **Charley Pride** was the first Black artist to win the Country Music Association's Entertainer of the Year Award. In 2000, he was the first Black inductee into the Country Music Hall of Fame. In 1974, **Stevie Wonder** became the first Black artist to win the Grammy Award for album of the year.

Name: Date:

Activity: Locating Information

Directions: Use the information from the reading selection to complete the charts.

"Who Am I?" Statement	African American Athlete
1. I competed in the 1936 Olympics. I was the first American to win four Olympic gold medals.	
2. I competed in the 1988 Olympics. I was the first American woman to win an Olympic gold medal in the long jump and the heptathlon.	
3. In 1908, I was the first African American to win the world heavyweight boxing title.	
4. July 6, 1957, I was the first Black tennis player to win the women's singles tennis title at Wimbledon and the first African American to win a championship.	
5. I was the first African American to play Major League Baseball in 1947.	
6. We were two NBA superstars on the 1992 basketball "Dream Team" that won the Olympic gold medal.	

"Who Am I?" Statement	African American Entertainer
1. We received the Oscars for leading actor and actress in 2002, the first time both Oscars were awarded to African Americans.	
2. In 1939, I performed for a crowd of 75,000 at the Lincoln Memorial.	
3. In 1974, I was the first Black artist to win a Grammy Award for album of the year.	
4. In 1940, I was the first African American to win an Oscar.	
5. In 1971, I was the first Black artist to win the Country Music Association's Entertainer of the Year Award.	
6. In 1956, I was the first Black star of a national TV show.	

Science, Math, and Literature

Many African Americans have demonstrated exceptional achievements in science, math, and literature. We can only list a few here.

Science

George Washington Carver is considered the most prominent Black scientist of the early Twentieth Century. He promoted alternative crops to cotton and methods to prevent soil depletion. From 1915 to 1923, he discovered over three hundred uses for peanuts, including chili sauce, shampoo, shaving cream, and glue. He received numerous honors for his work, including the Spingarn Medal of the NAACP.

Mae C. Jemison was the first African American woman in space.

Frederick McKinley Jones developed refrigeration equipment, receiving over 40 patents for refrigeration. In the 1930s, he invented the **Thermo King**, an automatic refrigerated air-cooling unit for trucks, trains, ships, and planes, which helped in the preservation of food. The invention allowed people to eat fresh food year round. In 1991, he was the first African American to receive the National Medal of Technology.

In 1992, **Mae C. Jemison**, a graduate of Cornell Medical School, and six other astronauts went into space on the space shuttle *Endeavor*. With this voyage, Jemison became the first African American woman in space. She now leads the 100-Year Starship Project. She was inducted into the National Women's Hall of Fame, National Medical Association Hall of Fame, and Texas Science Hall of Fame. She received the National Organization for Women's Intrepid Award and the Kilby Science Award.

Math

Katherine Johnson was a NASA mathematician. She used math to calculate the paths for the spacecraft in the *Mercury* and *Apollo* programs to orbit Earth and land on the Moon. She was instrumental in John Glenn's first orbit of the Earth and worked for the space program for 33 years. Johnson was awarded the Presidential Medal of Freedom, the Congressional Gold Medal, and was inducted into the National Women's Hall of Fame.

David Blackwell was a mathematician who worked in the areas of game theory and statistics. He earned a Ph.D. in mathematics and was the first Black inductee into the National Academy of Sciences. In 2012, President Obama awarded Blackwell the National Medal of Science.

Literature

Phillis Wheatley published *Poems on Various Subjects, Religious and Moral* in 1773. The book was the first ever written and published by an African American,

In 1859, **Harriet Wilson** published *Our Nig: Sketches in the Life of a Free Black*, which is believed to be the first African American novel to be published in the United States.

Edward P. Jones is known for his novels and short stories, which depict the effects of slavery in America before the Civil War. In 2004, his book *The Known World* won him the Pulitzer Prize for Fiction.

Toni Morrison is best known for her book *Beloved*. Morrison won the Pulitzer Prize for her book in 1988. She was awarded the Nobel Prize in Literature in 1993.

Name: Date:

Activity: Textual Evidence

Directions: Use information from the reading selection to answer the questions. Support your answers with specific details and examples.

1. Who was the first African American to receive the National Medal of Technology?

Answer:

2. Who was the first African American woman in space?

Answer:

3. Who was the first African American inducted into the National Academy of Sciences?

Answer:

4. Who was the first African American to write and publish a book?

Answer:

African Americans and Politics

African Americans have risen to influence in politics and have held important positions in the government since the Reconstruction Era.

Thurgood Marshall, first African American Supreme Court justice

Congress

The first African American to serve in Congress was **Hiram Revels** of Mississippi. Revels began his service in the U.S. Senate when he was sworn in on February 25, 1870 to fill a vacant seat. The first African American Representative elected to Congress was **Joseph Rainey** of South Carolina. He began his service in the House of Representatives when he was sworn in on December 12, 1870. The first African American woman elected to Congress was **Shirley Chisholm** of New York. She was elected to the House of Representatives in 1968. The first African American woman elected to the Senate was **Carol Moseley-Braun** of Illinois. She was elected to the Senate in 1992.

Advisors and Cabinet Members

African Americans have served as presidential advisors and in key political policy-making positions. On January 13, 1966, President Lyndon B. Johnson appointed the first African American cabinet member, making **Robert C. Weaver** head of the Department of Housing and Urban Development (HUD). The agency develops and implements national housing policies and enforces fair housing laws.

Starting in 1987, **Colin Powell** served as the first African American National Security Advisor under President Ronald Reagan. On January 20, 2001, Powell was appointed the first African American Secretary of State by President George W. Bush. In 2005, **Condoleezza Rice** became the first African American woman Secretary of State under President George W. Bush.

Supreme Court

In the judicial branch, three African Americans have served on the U.S. Supreme Court: **Thurgood Marshall**, **Clarence Thomas**, and **Ketanji Brown Jackson**. On October 2, 1967, Thurgood Marshall took the judicial oath of office for the U.S. Supreme Court, becoming the first Black person to serve on the Court. On April 7, 2022, Ketanji Brown Jackson became the first Black woman confirmed to the Supreme Court.

Governors and Mayors

Douglas Wilder was the first African American elected governor of a state. He was sworn in as governor of Virginia on January 13, 1990. **Carl B. Stokes** was the first African American elected mayor of a major United States city, serving in Cleveland, Ohio, from 1968 to 1971.

Executive Office

In 1848, **Frederick Douglass** became the first African American presidential candidate in the United States. On January 20, 2009, **Barack Hussein Obama** became the first Black American president. In January 2021, **Kamala D. Harris** became the first woman, the first Black American, and the first South Asian American to be elected Vice President of the United States.

Name:	Date:

Activity: Locating Information

Directions: Use information from the reading selection to complete the chart.

African Americans Enter Politics		
First African American . . .	**Date**	**Name**
1. To serve in United States Congress		
2. Elected to United States Congress		
3. Woman elected to United States House of Representatives		
4. Woman elected to United States Senate		
5. Presidential cabinet member		
6. National Security Advisor		
7. Secretary of State		
8. Woman to serve as Secretary of State		
9. To serve on United States Supreme Court		
10. Woman confirmed to the United States Supreme Court		
11. Governor of a state		
12. Mayor of a major city		
13. Presidential candidate		
14. Vice president of the United States		
15. President of the United States		

President Barack Obama

On January 20, 2009, Barack Hussein Obama II was inaugurated as the 44th President of the United States.

Early Life

Barack Obama was born in Honolulu, Hawaii, in 1961. His mother was a white American from Hawaii. His father was from Kenya, Africa. At age six, he moved to Jakarta, Indonesia. At the age of ten, Barack returned to Hawaii to live with his grandparents and continue his schooling. After graduating from Columbia University in 1983, Obama worked in Chicago as a community organizer, helping to rebuild communities impacted by the closing of local steel plants. In 1988, he attended Harvard Law School. After graduating, he became a civil rights attorney and an academic, teaching constitutional law

Barack Hussein Obama II, the 44th President of the United States

at the University of Chicago Law School. In 1992, Obama married Michelle Robinson. They had two daughters. He was elected to the Illinois State Senate in 1996 and the U.S. Senate representing Illinois in 2004. He began his term on January 3, 2005.

First Term in Office

On February 10, 2007, Barack Obama announced his candidacy to become the Democratic Party's presidential nominee. On November 4, 2008, Barack Obama was elected President of the United States, receiving almost 10,000,000 more popular votes than his opponent, John McCain.

President Obama began his first term on January 20, 2009. He "inherited a troubled economic situation," often referred to as the **Great Recession**. On February 17, 2009, he signed into law the **American Recovery and Reinvestment Act** (ARRA), a $787 billion economic-growth package that addressed tax cuts, infrastructure, energy, education, health care, and social welfare programs, such as an expansion of unemployment benefits. On October 9, 2009, Obama was awarded the **Nobel Peace Prize**. He signed into law the **Affordable Care Act**, a plan to reform health care and cover millions of uninsured Americans, on March 23, 2010. On July 21, 2010, he signed the **Dodd-Frank Wall Street Reform and Consumer Protection Act**, which reformed regulations of banking and financial institutions and created a consumer protection bureau.

Obama signed the instrument of ratification for a new **START Treaty** with Russia on February 2, 2011. The treaty limited the number of nuclear warheads and strengthened the monitoring program between the two countries. On May 1, 2011, he approved the plan for special forces to raid the secret compound of **Osama bin Laden** and to kill the al Qaeda leader. Bin Laden was the mastermind behind the September 11, 2001, terrorist attacks on the United States.

Second Term in Office

On November 6, 2012, President Obama was re-elected to a second term in office. On July 14, 2015, the **Iran Nuclear Deal** was reached between Iran, the United States, and five other nations. The deal limited Iran's nuclear capabilities.

President Obama left office on January 20, 2017, with an approval rating of over 50 percent.

Name: Date:

Activity: Chronological Order

Directions: Use information from the reading selection to complete the timeline featuring events from President Obama's presidency. The first one is done for you.

Barack Obama

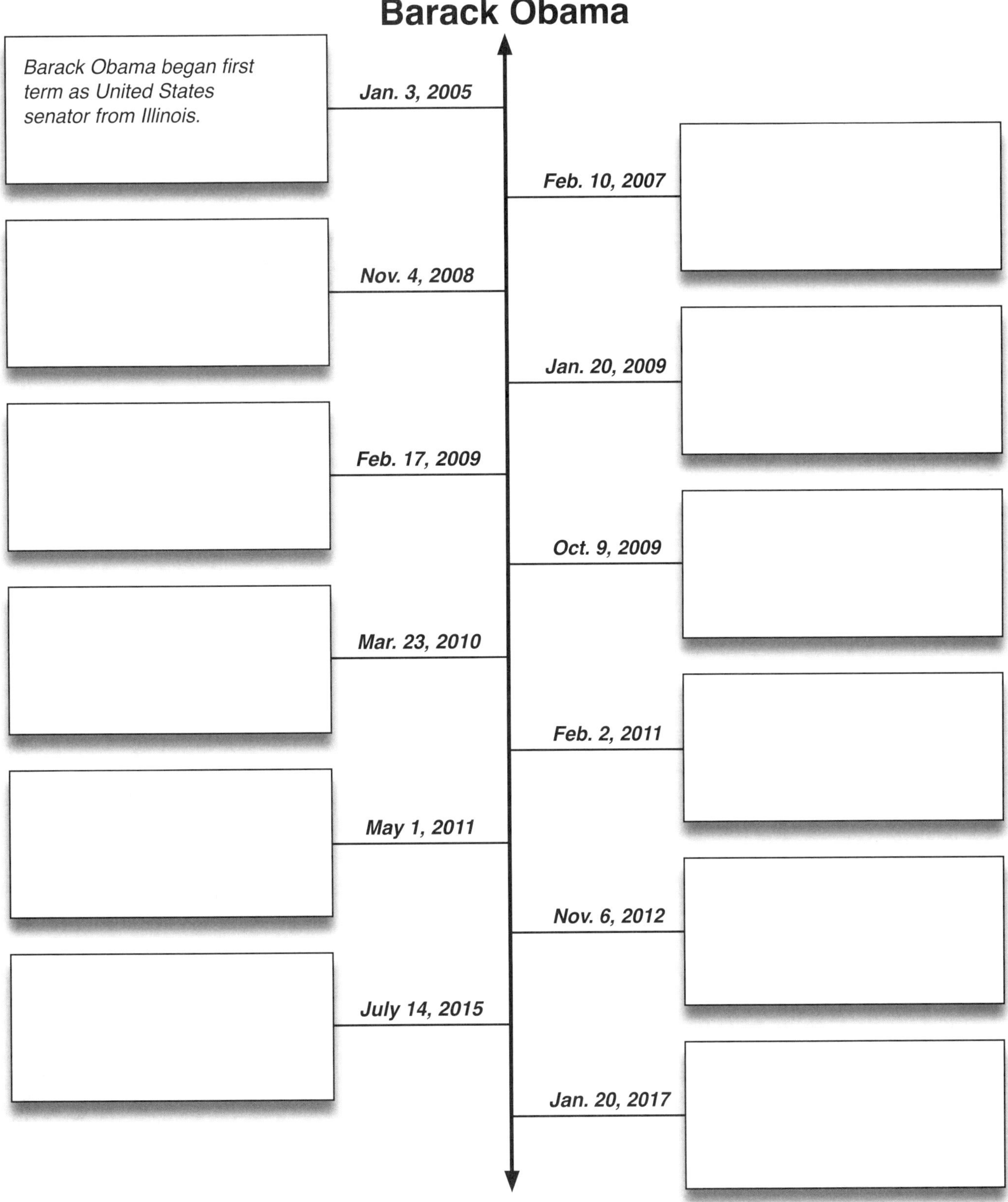

Vice President Kamala D. Harris

On January 21, 2021, Kamala Harris broke many records for "first" in American history. She became the first woman, the first Black American, and the first South Asian American to be elected Vice President of the United States.

Kamala D. Harris officially became the 49th vice president of the United States on January 20, 2021.

Early Life

Kamala Devi Harris was born on October 20, 1964, in Oakland, California. Her parents were immigrants. Kamala's mother was from India, and her father was from Jamaica.

Kamala went to kindergarten at Thousand Oaks Elementary School in Northern Berkeley. When Kamala was 12, her family moved to Montreal, Quebec, where she graduated from high school in 1981.

After high school, Kamala returned to the United States and attended Howard University in Washington, D.C. She graduated in 1986. She earned a law degree from the University of California, Hastings College of the Law in San Francisco in 1989. She was admitted to the California Bar in June 1990.

She married Doug Craig Emhoff in 2014 and has two stepchildren.

Early Political Career

Kamala Harris was elected the **attorney general** (chief law officer) for the state of California in 2010. She served as attorney general from 2011 to 2017. Harris was the first woman, African American, and South Asian American to be elected attorney general of California.

In 2016, she was elected to the United States Senate for the state of California. She was the first Indian American and second Black woman to serve as a senator. She served as senator from 2017 until 2021. Kamala focused on criminal justice reform during her time as senator.

Author Kamala Harris

Kamala Harris has written three books. In 2009, she published her first book *Smart on Crime: A Career Prosecutor's Plan to Make Us Safer.* Harris published two books in early 2019: *The Truths We Hold: An American Journey* and the children's book *Superheroes Are Everywhere.*

Executive Office

On January 21, 2019, during a Martin Luther King, Jr., Day interview, Harris announced her candidacy for President of the United States in the 2020 election. After participating in five Democratic presidential primary debates, she ended her campaign on December 3, 2019. Harris said her campaign did not have enough funds to continue an effective campaign. On March 8, 2020, Harris endorsed Joe Biden for president.

In August 2020 just before the Democratic presidential convention, Joe Biden, the leading candidate for the Democratic nomination for president, picked Harris as his vice-presidential candidate for the 2020 presidential election. Biden and Harris won the election in November over the **incumbent** (currently holding the office) Republican president and vice president, Donald Trump and Mike Pence. Harris officially became the 49th vice president of the United States on January 20, 2021.

Name: Date:

Activity: Recalling Information

Directions: Use information from the reading selection to complete the page.

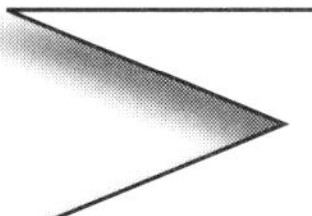 **Vice President
Kamala D. Harris** 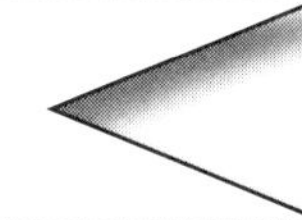

Multiple Choice

1. Where was Kamala Harris born?
   a. Orlando, Florida
   b. Chicago, Illinois
   c. Oakland, California
   d. Austin, Texas

2. Kamala Harris is...
   a. The first woman United States Vice President
   b. The first Black United States Vice President
   c. The first South Asian American United States Vice President
   d. All of the above

Fill in the Blanks

1. Harris officially became the 49th vice president of the United States on January 20, ________________.

2. In 2019, Harris published the children's book ___________________________________.

3. When Kamala was 12, her family moved to ___________________________________.

4. Harris was the first woman, first Black woman, and first South Asian American to be elected ___________________________ of California.

True or False

Write the word TRUE if the statement is correct. If the statement is false, write FALSE and underline the word or statement that makes the sentence incorrect. Write the correct answer in the space provided under each statement.

__________ 1. In 2010, Kamala Harris became the attorney general of Nevada.

__________ 2. Kamala Harris' full name is Kamala Devi Harris.

__________ 3. Kamala Harris' father was an immigrant from Kenya.

Black History Month

Dr. Carter G. Woodson is considered the "father of Black history."

The history of African Americans is a vital part of the history of our nation from exploration and settlement to the present day. Black History Month was created to honor the contributions of African Americans to the United States. It is a time to focus on the contributions of Black people from the early 1500s to African Americans living in the United States today.

Negro History Week

Carter G. Woodson, a historian, is considered the "father of Black history." In 1915, Carter G. Woodson and Jesse E. Moorland founded the Association for the Study of Negro Life and History (now known as the Association for the Study of African American Life and History, ASALH). The organization sponsored a national **Negro History Week** in 1926. It was a time to "highlight the history, lives, and contributions of Black Americans to American society." The second week of February was chosen as Negro History Week because it coincided with the birthday of Abraham Lincoln on February 12 and that of Frederick Douglass on February 14. The idea eventually grew in acceptance, and by the late 1960s, Negro History Week had evolved into what is now known as Black History Month.

Black History Month

In the 1960s, college students began calling for colleges to extend Negro History Week into a month-long celebration. During the 1976 United States bicentennial, President Gerald R. Ford officially recognized **Black History Month**. The president called upon Americans to "seize the opportunity to honor the too-often neglected accomplishments of Black Americans in every area of endeavor throughout our history." Black History Month is now celebrated outside of the United States in other countries as well, including Canada and the United Kingdom.

Black History Month Theme

Since 1976, every American president has designated February as Black History Month and endorsed a specific theme for the celebration. Recent themes include African Americans and the Civil War, Black Women in American Culture and History, and Civil Rights in America.

United States Postage Stamps

There have been many U.S. postage stamps over the years that celebrate Black History Month. In the past 70 years, over 100 accomplished Black Americans have been pictured on stamps. On April 7, 1940, the Post Office Department issued a stamp honoring African American educator **Booker T. Washington** as part of its Famous Americans series. It was the nation's first stamp to honor an African American. In 2022, the 45th stamp in the Black Heritage series was for **Edmonia Lewis**, the first African American and Native American sculptor to earn international recognition.

Name: ___________________________ Date: ___________________________

Activity: Compare and Contrast

Directions: Use information from the reading selection to complete the graphic organizer.

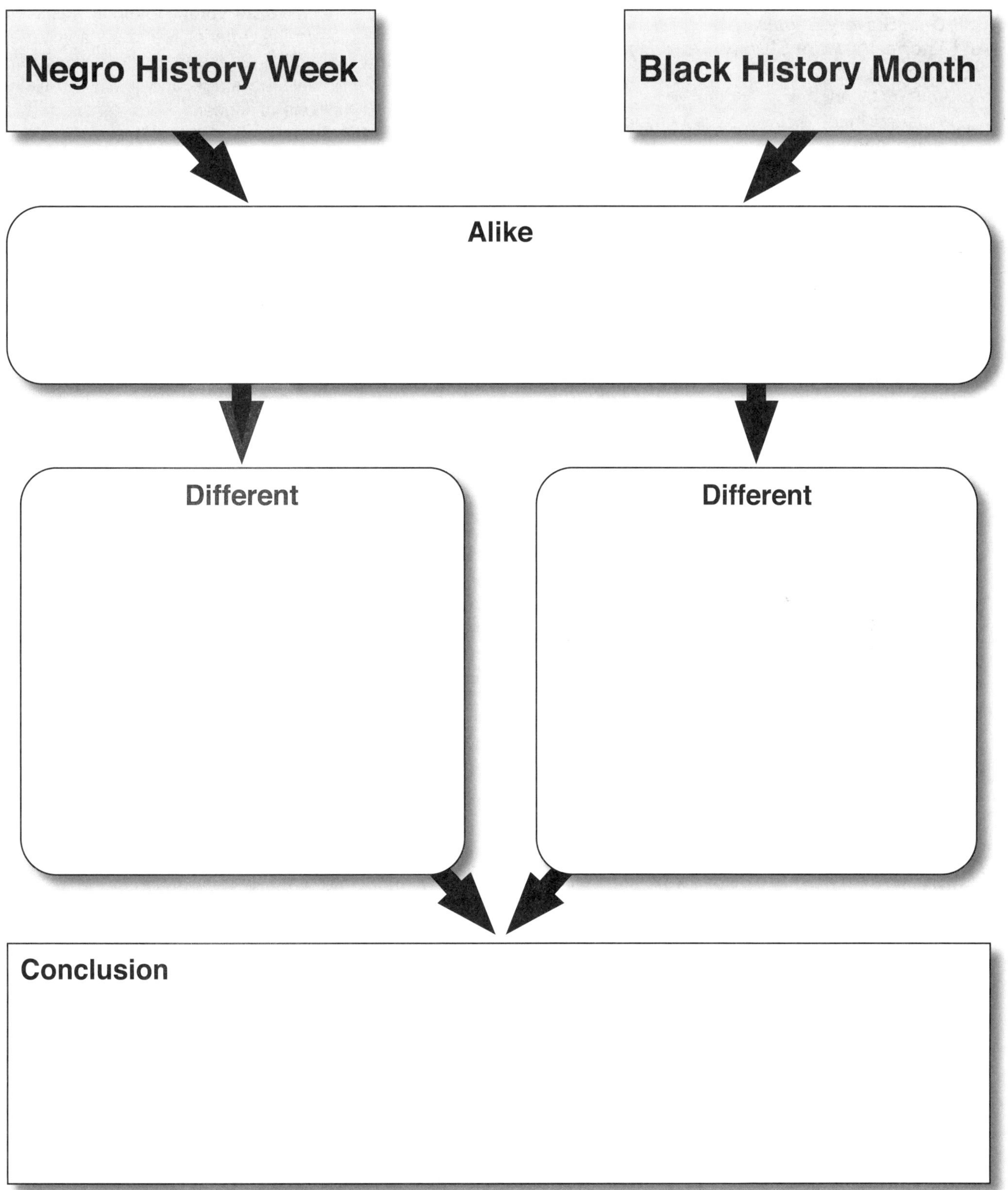

Answer Keys

Note: Some answers may vary. Suggested answers are given, but students may have other valid answers. Teacher check for appropriate responses.

Unit One: Slavery Begins
An Historical View of Slavery: Word Meaning (p. 3)
1. *slavery:* a system where one person is owned as property by another
   enslaved: made a slave, owned and forced to work against one's will
2. *Arab trade:* enslaved people transported to the Middle East and Asia and sold
   European trade: enslaved people transported to Europe, Central and South America, and the British colonies in North America and sold
3. *Christopher Columbus:* claimed the region now known as the West Indies for Spain
   Bartolomé de Las Casas: a Spanish landowner and priest responsible for the beginning of the importation of enslaved Africans to the Spanish colonies in the Caribbean as a way to spare the Native Americans used as slave labor; later rejected enslaving Africans too
4. *Portuguese Brazil:* a region under Portuguese rule that imported enslaved workers from Africa
   Palmares: a colony in Brazil where many enslaved Africans from Brazil escaped to from 1605 to 1694

Jamestown: Cause and Effect (p. 5)
Effects
1. In 1607, three ships sailed into the Chesapeake Bay. The 104 men and boys on board established a new settlement named Jamestown after King James I. The settlers built a fort along with several houses.
2. John Rolfe developed a type of tobacco the English liked. Soon the colony was sending shiploads of tobacco to England. There it became popular and sold for very high prices. The high price of tobacco created a demand for people to work in the fields. The indentured servant system was used to provide workers for the colony.
3. The *White Lion* brought 50 enslaved Africans to Jamestown. Twenty were sold as indentured servants. After their time of servitude ended, it is believed that they were freed. This event is considered by many to be the beginning of slavery in the colonies.

The Middle Passage: Central Idea and Key Details (p. 7)
Slave trade: the capturing, selling, and buying of enslaved Africans

Transatlantic slave trade: the selling of captured Africans by Europeans in and around the Atlantic Ocean. It included three routes, in which arms, textiles, and wine were shipped from Europe to Africa, enslaved people from Africa to the Americas, and sugar, coffee, and other raw materials from the Americas to Europe.
Middle Passage: was the stage of the Atlantic slave trade in which millions of Africans were transported to the Americas in ships as part of the triangular slave trade

The American Revolution: Locating Information (p. 9)
Activity 1: In 1775, Governor Dunmore of Virginia declared that any enslaved African or indentured servant who joined the British Army would be free. Enslaved Africans deserted the plantations and enlisted in the Royal Army. Many of the enslaved Africans working on Washington's plantation escaped to join the British Army.
Activity 2:
Alike: William Lee and James Armistead Lafayette were both enslaved Africans. Both were given their freedom after the Revolutionary War.
Different: William Lee was purchased by George Washington. Lee served as Washington's personal assistant. Washington freed Lee in his will. James Armistead Lafayette served as a spy for the Continental Army during the American Revolutionary War under the Marquis de Lafayette. In 1787, James was granted his freedom for service during the Revolution with help from Lafayette.

The Founding Documents: Textual Evidence (p. 11)
1. Founding documents define the framework and powers of the federal government.
2. The Declaration of Independence
   The Articles of Confederation
   The Constitution of the United States
3. The copy submitted to Congress by Thomas Jefferson called slavery an "abominable crime." Fearful of dividing the fragile new nation over the issue of slavery, the statement was removed.
4. It was agreed that the power to regulate slavery would be left to the individual states.
5. The Three-Fifths Compromise was reached for both taxation and representation. It declared "all other persons" (enslaved persons) would count as three-fifths of a person. A compromise was reached allowing the trade of enslaved Africans to continue another 20 years. Article IV, Section 2, of the Constitution known as the "Fugitive Slave Clause" declared states were to return "fugitives" to the state from which they fled.

Two Remarkable African Americans: Locating Information (p. 13)

Phillis Wheatley

Born: West Africa, 1753, Died: 1784

Accomplishments: first Black woman in America to have her writing published; age of 14 wrote her first poem, "To the University of Cambridge, in New England"; age 17, her poetry book published; during the Revolutionary War, wrote poem "His Excellency General Washington"

Benjamin Banneker

Born: colony of Maryland, 1731, Died: 1806

Accomplishments: In his early 20s, designed and built first wooden clock of its type in the colonies; learned astronomy; surveyed the land for the United States capital city of Washington, D.C.; published an almanac from 1792 to 1797; corresponded with Thomas Jefferson

Unit Two: The War to End Slavery

Events Leading to War: Event and Effect (p. 15)

Event 1: Plantation owners expanded production of cotton, which required more workers.

Event 2: Missouri was added to the United States as a slave state and Maine as a free state.

Event 3: Protected Northern factories by taxing imports from Europe so people in the United States would buy goods produced in the United States. The South had few factories, so they were forced to buy goods produced in the North or pay the tax on imported goods. They felt they were harmed by the high tariff.

Event 4: Fugitive Slave Act required enslaved people who had escaped to be returned to their owners even if they were found in a free state.

Event 5: Kansas-Nebraska Act created two new territories allowing slavery if the people chose.

The Abolitionist Movement: Compare and Contrast (p. 17)

Slavery

Abolitionists: people who wanted to end slavery

Abolitionist Movement: an organized effort to end the practice of slavery in the United States.

Abolitionists

Sojourner Truth: born into slavery in New York, ran away and an abolitionist family paid for her freedom, advocated for a Negro State in the west on public lands, traveled the country telling people what it was like to be enslaved, recruited Black soldiers to fight for the Union, spoke out for women's rights

Frederick Douglass: born into slavery in Maryland, escaped to New York City, wrote book about his life called *Narrative of the Life of Frederick Douglass*, published an anti-slavery newspaper known as *The North Star*

Abolitionists

William Lloyd Garrison: a white Northerner, associated with the American Colonization Society, an organization that believed free Blacks should move to a territory on the west coast of Africa. Published an anti-slavery newspaper, *The Liberator.*

Harriet Beecher Stowe: a white American author who published the book called *Uncle Tom's Cabin* about the difficult lives of enslaved African Americans.

The Underground Railroad: Textual Evidence (p. 19)

1. required all citizens to help catch fugitive slaves
2. a network of people, African Americans as well as whites, offering shelter and aid to freedom seekers escaping from the South to get to free states in the North and to Canada
3. Conductors guided freedom seekers along the freedom trails. Station masters hid fugitives and arranged safe passage to freedom.
4. He interviewed each freedom seeker passing through Philadelphia and kept thorough and detailed records. Published the book *The Underground Railroad.*

Dred Scott to John Brown: Summarizing (p. 21)

Dred Scott v. Sandford Supreme Court Case

1857 United States Supreme Court case. Dred Scott was an enslaved man bought in Missouri, a slave state, and taken into a free territory. The court said that Scott was not a citizen of Missouri or the United States. The Court also ruled that Congress lacked the power to ban slavery in the United States.

The Lincoln-Douglas Debates

The two held a series of debates in 1858. Douglas argued it was the right of the citizens of a territory to permit or prohibit slavery. Lincoln argued African Americans were included under the rights given by the Declaration of Independence. While it was constitutional to allow slavery to spread to the territories, he believed this would lead to slavery being legal everywhere. He believed only the federal government had the power to abolish slavery. The debates drew national attention to slavery and the rights of Black Americans.

John Brown's Raid on Harpers Ferry

Brown attacked Harpers Ferry on October 16, 1859. He planned to free the enslaved people in the area and move down the Appalachian Mountains, building an army as he went. Brown and his men were captured, and Brown was hanged for treason.

Summary

Between 1857 and 1859, several events deepened the divide between the North and the South. The *Dred Scott v. Sandford* Supreme Court ruling in 1857 angered many Northerners because the Court also ruled that Congress lacked power to ban slavery in the United States. The Lincoln-Douglas Debates in 1958 drew national attention to slavery and the rights of Black Americans. John Brown's Raid on Harpers Ferry in 1859 convinced Southerners abolitionists would use any means, including violence, to end slavery. Each event propelled the nation closer to war.

Secession Divides the Nation: Locating Information (p. 23)

Border States
1. Missouri   2. Kentucky   3. West Virginia
4. Maryland   5. Delaware

Southern States Secede

States' Rights: The leaders in the South believed individual states should have more control over laws than the federal government. They did not want a stronger national government that would make the same laws for all the states.

Slavery: The South believed in the practice of slavery. They were afraid that the Northern states would vote to make slavery illegal in all the states.

New States: The leaders of the Southern states wanted to extend slavery into all new states. Northern states wanted to end the expansion of slavery.

President Abraham Lincoln: Lincoln was against the expansion of slavery into new states and wanted a strong federal government, two things the South did not agree with.

The Emancipation Proclamation: Opinions (p. 25)

Purpose of the War

Lincoln: save the union

Congress: save the Union

Slavery

Lincoln: Border states should free slaves

Border States: did not want slavery to end

Colony on Île à Vache

Lincoln: wanted to establish a colony for formerly enslaved people

African Americans: wanted to stay in United States, did not want to set up a colony elsewhere

Enslaved African Americans

Lincoln: didn't believe the Constitution gave him the power to abolish slavery in all the states

Frederick Douglass: wanted complete and immediate emancipation with full civil rights of all enslaved men and women

African Americans and the War Effort: Key Details (p. 27)

Contraband of War: Union armies considered freedom-seeking enslaved people as contraband of war. They were used as a work force for the troops.

Militia Act of July 1886: The law allowed President Abraham Lincoln to employ Blacks "for any military or naval service for which they may be found competent."

Bureau of Colored Troops: created by the United States War Department on May 22, 1863, for "the organization of colored troops"

General Orders No. 14: Jefferson Davis signed the General Orders No. 14, also known as the Negro Soldier Law, on March 13, 1865, allowing Black men to serve in the Confederate Army, but fighting ended before Blacks were allowed to serve.

Unit Three: Reconstruction Brings Change
Reconstruction Amendments: Cause and Effect (p. 29)

Thirteenth Amendment: freed all enslaved people within the United States and made slavery illegal forever.

Fourteenth Amendment: granted citizenship to men over 21 who had been born or naturalized in the United States; guaranteed due process and equal protection under the law to all citizens.

Fifteenth Amendment: gave African American men all rights of citizenship, including right to vote

The Freedmen's Bureau: Key Details (p. 31)

Detail 1: established by Congress on March 3, 1865

Detail 2: provided food, shelter, clothing, and medical services; opened hospitals and provided medical assistance to millions of people both Black and white.

Detail 3: establishment of a public education system in the South for formerly enslaved people

Black Codes to Civil Rights Acts: Textual Evidence (p. 33)

1. Southern states were opposed to the Civil Rights Bill. In 1865 and early 1866, the new Southern state legislatures passed a series of laws based on the slave codes. These new laws were called Black Codes. The laws were designed to continue providing cheap sources of labor for Southerners and were based on the belief that African Americans were inferior beings.
2. The Southern states were opposed to the Civil Rights Act. In the 1890s, Southern state legislatures enacted a new form of Black Codes, called Jim Crow Laws. The laws required "separate but equal" status for African Americans. The laws were designed to keep Black and white people apart in public places such as theaters, restaurants, hotels, schools, parks, trains, streetcars, and even restrooms.

Sharecropping: Cause and Effect (p. 35)

1: The order was a temporary plan granting each freed family 40 acres of land on the islands and coastal regions of Georgia. Formerly enslaved people began to expect "Forty Acres and a Mule" after the war.
2: Johnson ordered all land under federal control to be returned to the previous owners. Freedmen and whites living on the land could sign a labor contract with the previous landowners or be evicted from the land.
3: There was an economic catastrophe and widespread unemployment in the South. African Americans began moving to northern cities.

African Americans Move West: Key Details (p. 37)
Estevanico: 1528 accompanied Cabeza de Vaca on his exploration of southwestern United States. He was the first African-born person in the New World.
York: 1804 accompanied Clark on the Lewis and Clark Expedition of 1804; first enslaved African American to cross the continent and see the Pacific Ocean.
Jim Beckwourth: 1850 discovered a way through the Sierra Nevada Mountains to California now known as the Beckwourth Pass.
Nat Love: most famous Black cowboy
Mary Fields: first African American female star route mail carrier, delivering mail by stagecoach
Bass Reeves: 1875 became a deputy U.S. marshal
Lieutenant Henry Flipper: the first African American to graduate from West Point, served as a buffalo solider in U.S. Cavalry as an officer
Benjamin Singleton: helped establish African American settlements in Kansas

African Americans Who Made a Difference: Locating Information (p. 39)
Blanche Kelso Bruce: In 1864, started the first school for African American children in Missouri in Hannibal; in 1874, first African American to serve a full term in the U.S. Senate
Booker T. Washington: First leader of the Tuskegee Normal and Industrial Institute; dined at the White House with President Theodore Roosevelt
George Washington Carver: found new ways to process peanuts, soybeans, and sweet potatoes; made these important crops in the South
Fannie Barrier Williams: In 1896, helped found the National League of Colored Women; in 1909, helped found the National Association for the Advancement of Colored People (NAACP); spoke and wrote about women's rights and discrimination against African Americans

Unit Four: The Twentieth Century
The Jazz Age: Key Details (p. 41)
Age of Jazz: the 1920s when jazz music became very popular across the United States; originated in the African American communities of New Orleans, Louisiana; roots in spirituals, blues, and ragtime; "blues" was a type of music developed by African Americans that combined elements of spirituals, traditional African music, and work songs in a call and response format
Bessie Smith: most popular female blues singer during the 1920s; was known as the "Empress of the Blues"
Louis Armstrong: an African American trumpeter and vocalist; considered one of the most influential figures in jazz; joined King Oliver's Creole Jazz Band; led his own band and made records

Twentieth Century Wars: Locating Information (p. 43)
World War I: 1914–1918; assassination of Austrian Archduke Franz Ferdinand; 369th Infantry in France engaged 91 days of combat, awarded Croix de Guerre
World War II: 1939–1945; Axis Powers wanted to take over Europe and Asia; about one million African Americans served in the U.S. forces
Korean War: 1950–1953; stop North Korean communists from invading South Korea; approximately 600,000 African Americans served in the armed forces
Vietnam War: 1955–1975: stop the spread of communism in Vietnam; 300,000 African Americans served in Vietnam
Persian Gulf War: 1990–1991; liberate the country of Kuwait from Iraq; about 104,000 African Americans served in the Persian Gulf War

The Modern Civil Rights Era: Chorological Order (p. 45)
May 17,1954: *Brown v. Board of Education*
December 1, 1955: Rosa Parks was arrested in Montgomery, Alabama.
September 4, 1957: integration of Little Rock Central High School in Little Rock, Arkansas
February 1, 1960: sit-in at Woolworth's lunch counter in Greensboro, North Carolina
April 12, 1963: Dr. Martin Luther King, Jr., led a march in Birmingham, Alabama
August 28, 1963: over 200,000 people participated in the "March on Washington" demonstration
July 2, 1964: President Lyndon B. Johnson signed the Civil Rights Act of 1964.
October 14, 1964: Martin Luther King, Jr., was awarded the Nobel Peace Prize.
August 6, 1965: President Johnson signed the Voting Rights Act of 1965
April 4, 1968: Martin Luther King, Jr., was assassinated.
April 11, 1968: President Johnson signed the Civil Rights Act of 1968 (Fair Housing Act).

Unit Five: Achievements
Sports and Entertainment: Locating Information (p. 47)
African American Athlete
  1. Jessie Owens
  2. Jackie Joyner-Kersee
  3. Jack Johnson
  4. Althea Gibson
  5. Jackie Robinson
  6. Michael Jordan and Magic Johnson
African American Entertainer
  1. Denzel Washington and Halle Berry
  2. Marian Anderson
  3. Stevie Wonder
  4. Hattie McDaniel
  5. Charley Pride
  6. Nat King Cole

Science, Math, and Literature: Textual Evidence (p. 49)
1. Frederick McKinley Jones; developed refrigeration equipment, received over 40 patents for refrigeration; In 1991, first African American to receive the National Medal of Technology
2. Mae C. Jemison; first African American woman in space aboard the Space Shuttle *Endeavor* in 1992; inducted into the National Women's Hall of Fame, National Medical Association Hall of Fame and Texas Science Hall of Fame; received the National Organization for Women's Intrepid Award and the Kilby Science Award
3. David Blackwell; received a PhD in mathematics; in 2012, awarded National Medal of Science
4. Phillis Wheatley; published *Poems on Various Subjects, Religious and Moral* in 1773

African Americans and Politics: Locating Information (p. 51)
African Americans Enter Politics
1. Hiram Revels, 1870
2. Joseph Rainey, 1870
3. Shirley Chisholm, 1968
4. Carol Moseley-Braun,1992
5. Robert C. Weaver, 1966
6. Colin Powell, 1987
7. Colin Powell, 2001
8. Condoleezza Rice, 2005
9. Thurgood Marshall, 1967
10. Ketanji Brown Jackson, 2022
11. Douglas Wilder, 1990
12. Carl B. Stokes, 1968
13. Frederick Douglass, 1848
14. Kamala D. Harris, 2021
15. Barack Hussein Obama, 2009

President Barack Hussein Obama: Chronological Order (p. 53)
Jan. 3, 2005: began first term as United States senator for Illinois
Feb. 10, 2007: announced his candidacy to become the Democratic Party's presidential nominee.
Nov. 4, 2008: elected President of the United States
Jan. 20, 2009: began his first term as president
Feb. 17, 2009: signed into law the American Recovery and Reinvestment Act
Oct. 9, 2009: awarded Nobel Peace Prize
Mar. 23, 2010: signed into law the Affordable Care Act
Feb. 2, 2011: signed START Treaty with Russia
May 1, 2011: Approved killing al Qaeda leader, Osama bin Laden
Nov. 6, 2012: re-elected to a second term
July 14, 2015: Iran Nuclear Deal reached
Jan. 20, 2017: left office

Vice President Kamala D. Harris: Recalling Information (p. 55)
Multiple Choice
1. c   2. d
Fill in the Blanks
1. 2021
2. *Superheroes Are Everywhere*
3. Montreal, Quebec (Canada)
4. attorney general
True or False
1. False, California
2. True
3. False, Jamaica

Black History Month: Compare and Contrast (p. 57)
Alike: celebrated in February to focus on the contribution of Black people throughout the history of America
Different:
Negro History Week: organized in 1926 by Carter G. Woodson and Jesse E. Moorland, founders of the Association for the Study of Negro Life and History. The second week of February was chosen as "Negro History Week"; focused on the history of African Americans in the United States
Black History Month: Some colleges extended the week to a month in the 1960s. President Gerald R. Ford officially recognized Black History Month during the country's 1976 bicentennial; focus attention on the contributions of African Americans to the United States; celebrated outside of the United States in other countries, each year celebration has different theme
Conclusion:
The history of African Americans is a vital part of the history of our nation from exploration and settlement to the present day. "Negro History Week" for the purpose of promoting the study of Black history was founded in 1926 by Carter G. Woodson and the Association for the Study of Negro Life and History (ASNLH). The second week of February was chosen as "Negro History Week." "Negro History Week" has evolved into what is now known as Black History Month. President Gerald R. Ford officially recognized Black History Month during the country's 1976 bicentennial. The purpose was to honor the accomplishments of Black Americans in United States history. Each year the celebration has a different theme. Black History Month is now celebrated outside of the United States in other countries, including Canada and the United Kingdom